**BOA**

EDITIONS LTD

PERMANENT EXHIBIT

# PERMANENT EXHIBIT

## MATTHEW VOLLMER

ESSAYS

AMERICAN READER SERIES, NO. 31

BOA EDITIONS, LTD. • ROCHESTER, NY • 2018

First Edition
18  19  20  21  7  6  5  4  3  2  1

For information about permission to reuse any material from this book, please
contact The Permissions Company at www.permissionscompany.com or e-mail
permdude@gmail.com.

Publications by BOA Editions, Ltd.—a not-for-profit corpo-
ration under section 501 (c) (3) of the United States Internal
Revenue Code—are made possible with funds from a variety
of sources, including public funds from the Literature Program
of the National Endowment for the Arts; the New York State
Council on the Arts, a state agency; and the County of Monroe,
NY. Private funding sources include the Lannan Foundation;
the Max and Marian Farash Charitable Foundation; the Mary
S. Mulligan Charitable Trust; the Rochester Area Community
Foundation; the Ames-Amzalak Memorial Trust in memory of Henry Ames, Semon
Amzalak, and Dan Amzalak; and contributions from many individuals nationwide.
See Colophon on page 172 for special individual acknowledgments.

Cover Art: "Eclipso" by Eliash Strongowski
Cover Design: Sandy Knight
Interior Design and Composition: Richard Foerster
Manufacturing: McNaughton & Gunn
BOA Logo: Mirko

Library of Congress Cataloging-in-Publication Data

Names: Vollmer, Matthew, author.
Title: Permanent exhibit / by Matthew Vollmer.
Description: First edition. | Rochester, NY : BOA Editions, 2018. | Series:
  American reader series ; No. 31
Identifiers: LCCN 2018015164 (print) | LCCN 2018018813 (ebook) | ISBN
  9781942683698 (ebook) | ISBN 9781942683681 (pbk. : alk. paper)
Classification: LCC PS3622.O6435 (ebook) | LCC PS3622.O6435 A6 2018
(print) |
  DDC 814/.6—dc23
LC record available at https://lccn.loc.gov/2018015164

BOA Editions, Ltd.
250 North Goodman Street, Suite 306
Rochester, NY 14607
www.boaeditions.org
*A. Poulin, Jr., Founder (1938–1996)*

*for my friends*
*for my family*
*for those I do not yet know*
*and for those I never will*

# CONTENTS

9    Status Update

10    Hatchling

12    Last Blood

15    Robocall

17    Can't Feel My Face

19    33rd Balloon

22    Fool's Gold

24    Top Secret

27    Holy Hours

30    Bring Me the Head of Geraldo Rivera

33    Well of Souls

36    Out of Lives

40    Land of Enchantment

44    Signs of the Times

47    Stay Woke

51    Trick-or-Treat

55    Night Thoughts

59    Hands Up

62    Sinkhole

67    Spoiler Alert

71    Observatorium

75    Precious Metals

78    Permanent Exhibit

82    Treasure Box

85    Blood Soup

89    Stormbox

93    Gong Bang Cleanse

97    Brain Bank

101   Game Day

106   Eye of the Storm

110   Source Material

113   Cult Hymn

117   The Subordinate Fragment

121   We All Go into the Dark

137   Black Magic

141   Tiger Moth

145   Inferno

147   Fat Kid

151   Heron

156   The New You

160   Liftoff

•

168   *Acknowledgments*

169   *About the Author*

172   *Colophon*

# STATUS UPDATE

2016 and homes are still being raided for marijuana. Tropical Smoothie Cafe opened in Blacksburg today. Another black man was shot by police. I can't believe I'm running the dishwasher again. My bike can't ride itself. I miss the ocean. My closest family members are in Wyoming, which is possibly the most beautiful state ever created. I saw a baby deer nursing from its mother today in the middle of the road. I ate a slice of pizza big enough to wrap around my face. Ernest Becker's DENIAL OF DEATH is a good book. My best friends don't live next door. But my neighbor brought me a piece of junk mail and laughed at the look on my face because I was sure she would be a proselytizer. I don't understand all the *New Yorker* jokes. A chipmunk lives in my basketball goal. Earth is a planet I live on. Time to watch TV with wife.

# HATCHLING

Today, I watched a video of a black man who had been shot by a white police officer with the volume down because I didn't want my son to see the black man's blood-soaked shirt. I didn't want to see it, either, but I kept watching. I didn't turn the volume up when my son left the room, and I didn't listen to a press conference given by the mother of another black man who had been shot dead by a white policeman. I didn't read any comments. I wondered if words could change any mind that wasn't already disposed to changing, and remembered that Lao Tzu had once written, "Those who are stiff and rigid are the disciples of death. Those who are soft and yielding are the disciples of life." I picked up my phone, checked Instagram. I added words to a manuscript and wondered why anyone in their right mind—or wrong—would ever read it. I went upstairs to get a power strip and came back downstairs with something else, went back upstairs and then down again empty-handed, and imagined a future where I couldn't recognize myself in the mirror. I remembered to put ointment on the bumps on my arms caused by a mild skin condition I am just vain enough to half-heartedly manage. I read something about a presidential candidate who, according to an "insider," never wanted to be president, but wanted to finish at a solid second place, so as to increase his popularity. I thought about this guy who lives in my neighborhood, a retired financial analyst who challenged me to find anything about him at all on the Internet because it just isn't there, and who claims that there's an impending economic collapse because banks are playing with pretend money and soon the billionaires will be buying up land like crazy and jacking up the prices, which means that non-billionaires need to band together and buy land so that when the meltdown comes they can manage local foods/agriculture. I looked out my kitchen window at my neighbor's lush garden, for which she won't accept compliments, due to the amount of weeds she's neglected to pull, and acknowledged to myself how it's been so long since I've grown anything, and how there are zucchinis from that neighbor's garden in my fridge, and how they'll probably go bad because honestly I can't say that I'm that big a fan of squash no matter how roasted and/or cheese-coated. Then, when my wife finished a string of texts by sending me, inexplicably, a chicken emoji, I did the only thing I could do: I filled up the whole text box with a square halo of rooster heads orbiting a line of baby chicks with their wings out, sitting in the bottom halves of their broken, just-hatched eggs.

# LAST BLOOD

Woke up this morning to an email from Australia; a friend of mine sent me a video of his two-year-old asking me if I had feelings. Turns out? I do. My son's former soccer coach—a black man from Georgia, who some parents complained about because he insisted that their eleven-year-old boys run Manchester United drills—came out yesterday as gay, and I asked him if, to celebrate, he'd FedEx me an Oreo cookie pie, which is a dessert he made and delivered to our house last year when my wife was recuperating from major surgery, back when she'd been sent so many flower bouquets the sight of them made her sick. I forgot—and will likely forget again—to look up the name of the blue flower I keep seeing along the back roads of rural southwestern Virginia. I should know this flower, probably. It's everywhere, along with purple clover buds and the ivory spray of Queen Anne's Lace. Once, for an elementary school project, I gathered flowers and pressed them between paper towels inside volumes of World Book encyclopedias stacked on top of each other and then drew a grid and taped each dried, smashed, dead flower inside one of the squares, wrote the name of the flower beside it, laminated the whole thing, and submitted it for evaluation. Whatever grade I got I owe partly to the chemist William Farish, who, during the Industrial Revolution, developed our current system of grading—a method that allowed him to process more students and thereby increase his salary. How do you grade 200 drum-beating students? That's a question a cellist I know will have to answer next spring, when he teaches a new experiential art class. On my way to meet him for coffee yesterday, I passed a man on the street who was talking to himself. Another guy who noticed him shot me a glance. I pretended I wasn't concerned. A massage therapist I know has a patient who requests that the therapist not play Native American flute music, because it causes said patient to imagine that a peeping Tom is at the window. I wanted to think that this particular patient was stupid or paranoid, but I too am guilty of tricking myself into thinking things might happen that don't, like strangers yanking pistols from the waistbands of their pants and shooting me in the head. I don't own a gun, but when I was a kid, I found a stick shaped vaguely like a semiautomatic, and carried it around for weeks. I also held a Fisher-Price tape recorder to a television set so that I could record a movie review of *Rambo: First Blood Part II*—which featured a scene where a gunman fired round upon round of bullets into the river pool where Sylvester Stallone was hiding, submerged—because at that age there was little I loved more than the sound of a machine gun. Now I'm the kind of father who gleefully runs over pedestrians while playing *Grand Theft Auto V* and shames his son for being a failure at cleaning up spilled Legos; the snow shovel he used to scoop up 95% of them is still on the floor, along with the dinky spaceship he built. I think he could be a little more ambitious. For instance, there's a replica of Noah's Ark, engineered to the Bible's exact specifications, which just opened for business in Kentucky. I'd like to see it. I imagine standing in a line of granpaws and meemaws with concealed carry permits, telling their grandkids that without that long-ago Ark they wouldn't be here. That we humans now can't imagine how wicked the world used to be. I don't know what to think about that; it's hard to imagine one worse than we have. I do know that I'd like to continue living as I have, without getting shot in the head. But part of me can't help thinking: *it's only a matter of time.*

# ROBOCALL

I want a medal because I woke up wanting to tell my wife I think she gets more beautiful every day but didn't because commenting on her appearance makes her self-conscious. During the night, something bit me on the backside and now I have to rub cortisone on a quarter-sized welt on my left cheek. I had a dream that I was looking over a precipice into a room filled with water and I wanted to jump but was hesitant, which was good because it turned out the room wasn't actually filled with water: a tub in a nearby room had overflowed and it was only a puddle, which disappointed me, so I got a bucket and by god I was gonna fill up that room with water, at least until my wife asked me to stop because the floors were stained bad enough as they were. Also, while I was asleep, five police officers were shot and killed by a sniper who died when police blew him up with a bomb-deploying robot. According to the *Mirror*, sex robots may be the biggest tech trend of 2016. I'd rather think about sex bots than death bots, though there's something disturbing about the guy from that *Men's Health* article I read who has a human-sized doll he screws, and whose vagina he likes to remove and then "walk around with." The father of a kid on my son's soccer team—a professor of robotics, a guy from Rome—shouts words of encouragement for his son in Italian and addresses the boy as "Pizzolino"; when one of us finally asked what it meant, he said, sheepishly, "little penis." The landline rang today and like an insane person expecting a different result, I answered it, and once again, it was the automated guy who begins every call with the exclamation "Seniors!" which made me wonder: does he call because I have a landline or because I'm over forty—and does one of those explain why I get so much mail from AARP? The women I've befriended in the last five or so years whose company I enjoy the most— an editor, a retired schoolteacher, a retired professor of religion, and a retired Sunday School teacher—are all over the age of sixty-five, which makes me wonder: am I old or just looking for a mother figure? My father called from Yellowstone to tell me about two discoveries: one, whenever he made a squeak by blowing air through his tightly pressed lips, female mule deer came running, and two, he'd read an article about how the THC in marijuana could reverse memory loss, which made him inquire about whether or not I might have any connections. I suggested that he pay Colorado a visit. What I forgot to say, and what I would've said, if I'd thought he was serious: if you find anything good, save some for me.

# CAN'T FEEL MY FACE

Florida's toxic algae bloom smells, according to a boat sales-man, like "hundreds of dead animals that have been baking in the sun for weeks." Meanwhile, in our backyard, the hy-drangea is blossoming. As is the tree—I'm not always good with names of things, especially in nature—where the pre-vious owners hung a furry orb held together by what appears to be strips of wicker; at first, I thought it was some kind of witch ball—at least that's the phrase that appeared in my head when I saw it. I've since been informed that the thing is supposed to be a supplier of material for bird nests. If that's true, few birds seem to like it; it's the same size it was four months ago. So, "witch ball" it shall remain. Speak-ing of witch balls, a friend of mine—a woman who, when I was a kid, convinced me that two bite marks on her arm were the result of an encounter with a vampire—sent me a string of Facebook chats about how she's making a medi-cine bag—for protection against evil—and how she did a rain dance and then it rained and that, recently, a vulture talked to her. I like the idea that such a vile-looking bird might have something to say, or have some kind of wisdom to dispense. Earlier, on my bike, I surprised a venue of vul-tures (that's what a group of them are called, I know this because I looked it up), as they were pecking at the bloody, fur-ratted rib cage of a dead deer: the explosion of black wings nearly caused me to swerve into a ditch. Later, as I walked behind a lawnmower, light-blotches appeared and disappeared in the shadow cast by a tree, depending on whether or not a cloud was passing in front of the sun, and I anticipated the satisfaction I knew I'd get from eyeballing a just-mowed lawn, and how this particular sensation might be explained in part because shorter, more uniform grass blades create a pleasing symmetry, but also because it allows me to bask in the illusion that I have restored order and—for now—staved off chaos, and thus death. I was happy, once I reentered the house, to hear Spotify playing "Can't Feel My Face," a song that leaked on my birthday in the year 2015 and is—at least in part—about the numbing effects of cocaine. The composer, Abęl Makkonen Tesfaye—otherwise known as "The Weeknd"—is the son of Ethiopian parents who immigrated to Toronto. A biologist I know—a man who grew up in a community of power plant workers in China and who has for a number of years been developing a vaccine to help smokers who want to quit—told me recently during a long car ride from a soccer tournament our sons had played in that he—the biologist—doesn't approve of Tesfaye's hair, which *Rolling Stone* described as having "its own distinct personality" and that the front portion is similar to a "flopped-over moose antler" and that the back resembles a baby octopus. Aside from the fact that Tesfaye sounds so much like Michael Jackson, his hair is my favorite thing about him, especially after I learned he doesn't do anything to it except give it a good wash now and then. He doesn't style it at all. The hair does what it does on its own. All Tesfaye has to do? Just leave it alone.

# 33RD BALLOON

As I descended at full speed into the valley, I imagined—
as I often do—a deer leaping into the road and knocking
me off my bike. I'd wreck, snap my neck, suffer paralysis,
or bleed out on the road, and expire. In the end, what startled me wasn't a deer but a rabbit—no bigger than a ham-
burger bun—on the road's shoulder, inches away from my
oncoming wheel. It darted into high grass. The phrase "vi-
ciously cute" appeared in my head. I remembered the "rabbit
scene" from the 1987 film *Summer School*, in which a rag-
tag group of underperforming high school students, led by
a young teacher played by Mark Harmon, take a field trip
to a petting zoo. The scene begins with Anna-Maria, the
sultry Italian exchange student, as she pets a white rabbit
with whom she appears to be smitten. Dave and "Chainsaw"—two loveable doofs who are obsessed with horror
movies, especially *The Texas Chain Saw Massacre*—come
running into view, screaming frantically. It appears, inexplicably, that maniacal rabbits have latched onto their faces
and won't let go. As Dave and Chainsaw struggle to free
themselves, the bloody flesh of their cheeks stretches, and
they scream even louder. Anna-Maria screams and throws
her rabbit to the ground. Dave and Chainsaw collapse, as
if dead, only to jump back up seconds later, bowing. Their
classmates clap. Anna-Maria, seeing now that the rabbits
were stuffed, is confused. "Why did you do that?" she asks.
Chainsaw says, "We did it for you, Anna-Maria," and she

says, "Ew, that's disgusting," pauses, and then adds, "I *love* it." Chainsaw explains that his bloody cheeks aren't really bloody, peels off a shred of latex, hands it to her, and says, "Keep it." For whatever reason, this particular scene proved inspirational to me as a kid, but I didn't have latex, so I mashed up bananas mixed with red food coloring and spread it on my face, donned a gray wig that used to belong to a woman in my family once known as "Aunt Maddie" and filmed myself miming the roar of a wild animal in time to the recording of a wild animal. The bananas worked well as homemade gore, maybe because mashed bananas—the sight and texture—are disgusting on their own, which is too bad, because it turns out I can't swallow a bite of banana until I've chomped it to sludge. For the last month or so, I've been paying weekly visits to the house of a retired professor of Contemporary American Literature, who claims that, in India, there are countless varieties of bananas, each of which make an American banana seem even more bland and boring than they are. I've never understood the appeal of a banana split. Neither has my son, who was recently disappointed in our choice of ice cream scooper; he will settle for nothing less than one with a lever that, when depressed, forces the scoop into the bowl. If, God forbid, my son should die before me, these are the kinds of everyday things—in addition to the pulsing pain-hole I would carry in my chest for as long as I lived—that would haunt me relentlessly. Those of us who have not lost a child are compelled by stories of those who have, especially when those children are the tragic victims of senseless violence; the world in which they exist, we understand, is a darkness we cannot penetrate. We are less interested, it seems, in the parents of children who committed those acts of violence, except to wonder, maybe: *what did they do wrong?* I think now of a letter written by a professor to the parents of the young man who, on April 16, 2007, chained the doors of a campus building shut, then went in and out of classrooms, firing nearly 400 rounds of ammunition, injuring 17, killing 32, and then shooting himself in the head. In the letter, the professor—who is a friend and who, years later, showed it to me—told the parents that their son had been a student in her class. She wrote to express sympathy but also to assure them that not everybody refused to include their son in the tragedy's final tally, and that on the 33rd day after the massacre, the day after university officials, during a silent ceremony, released 32 balloons, each one drifting skyward, and each accompanied by the tolling of a single bell, this professor and her graduate teaching assistant visited the building where the shooting had occurred. There, they released the 33rd balloon. I don't know why she did this, but I suspect it wasn't just because the shooter had been her student—it was a way to recognize that though he'd committed inconceivably monstrous acts of violence, though he had left immeasurable devastations in his wake, he had once been a baby, a boy, a son, a brother, and that, if he had rarely been understood by his family, he had certainly been loved, a truth that, even if it couldn't shine through the dark sorrow of their shame, might make it easier, sometimes, when having to say his name.

# FOOL'S GOLD

Astronomers discovered a large, Jupiter-like planet orbiting three suns. At the Cascades, an iconic local waterfall, a man dove into the plunge pool to save his son, somehow pushed the boy safely to shore, but never resurfaced himself, and drowned. When soccer player Cristiano Ronaldo—who pays his personal hairstylist to style the hair of his likeness at Madrid's "Museum of Wax"—suffered a game-ending injury during the 2016 Euro Cup, a moth landed on the bridge of his nose, and fluttered its wings; even so, Ronaldo—perhaps because he was so crushed—did not bother to brush it away. In an empty parking lot outside a movie theater, I watched a crow pecking at spilled popcorn—yellow kernels, vivid as tiny nuggets of gold—and thought: *lucky*. A friend of mine who knows how to hunt mushrooms and has a map in his head of neighborhood trees that produce the best ones—"chicken of the woods" is now in season—told me that some restaurants douse the trash in their dumpsters with gasoline to discourage homeless people from scavenging. As I cycled up a mountain road, I spotted a cup in a roadside ditch that said, "Eat like you mean it," and once I got home, I slathered a just-nuked corn dog with pimento cheese. At the Blacksburg farmer's market, Weathertop Farm displays a flip book of photographs that documents the trajectories of their chickens' lives, from little yellow puffs to stately white birds in orange crates to featherless bodies at a slaughterhouse. Decades ago, one of my cousins, who had been raised a vegetarian for health and religious reasons, informed me that she'd only eaten animal flesh once in her life—a single bite of fried chicken—after which she'd promptly thrown up, a proclamation she'd delivered proudly, as if her body's automatic rejection of meat was proof of a kind of innate and irrefutable purity. The ACLU wants to know if I think people's religious beliefs are oppressing others in my community but the quiz they sent via mail was too long, so I slid it sheepishly—albeit responsibly—into the recycling bin. The sight of the American flag, I'm unashamed to say, does not fill me with hope. Still, I can't get these lyrics—from the song "Helplessness Blues" by Fleet Foxes—out of my head: "I was raised up believing I was somehow unique / Like a snowflake distinct among snowflakes, unique in each way you can see / And now after some thinking, I'd say I'd rather be / A functioning cog in some great machinery serving something beyond me." The phrase "Fiddler's Green" may refer to an afterlife of perpetual mirth, an extrasolar colony in Robert A. Heinlein's *The Cat Who Walks Through Walls*, a regimental poem of the U.S. 2nd Calvary Regiment, or the community of newly and garishly unimaginative homes spaced too closely together and that surround the original block of houses built in the 1960s where my family lives, and that also block our view of the horse hill in the distance; whenever I see the brick columns that designate the edges of this neighborhood, and which are decorated with a capital F and a capital G, I can't help but think: "Fool's Gold." For the first time in ten years, I hit every light on Main Street while it was still green, and though I silently cheered every time I made it safely through another intersection, I was disappointed to have arrived at my destination so early, because it meant then I'd have more time than I knew how to kill.

# TOP SECRET

What once was more or less secret: the bunker beneath the Greenbrier Hotel in White Sulphur Springs, West Virginia, a 112,544-square-foot facility that includes eighteen dormitories, decontamination chambers, a power plant, a television production area and audio recording booths, a clinic with twelve hospital beds, medical and dental operating rooms, a laboratory, a pharmacy, a cafeteria, and meeting rooms. Its three-foot thick concrete walls were designed to shelter the members of Congress during the aftermath of a nuclear holocaust, and until the Cuban Missile Crisis, when a trainload of congressmen from D.C. got halfway there, two of the four access points were disguised, simply, with signage: on a back door, the words "High Voltage" appeared, and on the sole elevator that dropped to bunker level, "Out of Order." Last fall, I mentioned to my Advanced Fiction class that a friend of mine claimed that Virginia Tech had a secret meditation room—that if you entered the elevator in Johnson Student Center and pressed the right buttons, in the right order, that this particular elevator would deliver you to a secret room between floors—and when my students begged to go see it, I had no choice but to lead an impromptu field trip. Once we arrived at the elevator and pressed the right buttons, in the right order—according to the directions one of the students had found on Reddit—we found ourselves in a place that didn't seem very secret or special at all: a room with an opaque skylight, a dingy lounge chair, carpet that desperately needed vacuuming, and a door that led—as far as we could tell by peering through its window—to a regular classroom. I visited Graceland once, and though I felt sort of like an intruder as I wandered past rooms with shag carpeting and mirrored walls and heavy drapes and stained glass panels of peacocks (the house struck me as quaintly modest in size, which granted the tour an intimacy I hadn't expected) I couldn't stop thinking about the part of the house I absolutely wasn't allowed to see: the upstairs rooms, which had been kept sealed like a vault ever since August of 1977, and to which nobody had ever had access, except for Priscilla, Lisa-Marie, Graceland's curator, and—because he had once been married to Lisa-Marie—Nicholas Cage, who purportedly sat on Elvis's throne and tried on one of the King's leather jackets. At the Magic Castle, a turn-of-the-20th-century mansion that is now an exclusive Hollywood club for magicians and magic enthusiasts, there's a piano room where invisible Irma—the ghost of a woman who used to live in the mansion—will play any song you request for a dollar; I tried to stump her by requesting an obscure hymn, but lo and behold, as the keys began to move—seemingly by themselves—I recognized the melody. Whenever my son used to ask me to reveal the secret to the one magic trick I could perform—making a quarter disappear, then pulling it out of his ear or spitting it out of my mouth—I always said, "I'll tell you when you're ten," and no matter how insistently he begged, I remained resolute, for years. Finally, on his tenth birthday, I woke him and said, "You know what day it is?" He did. "Okay," I said, "watch closely." I performed the trick again, slower than usual, taking my time to show him exactly how it was done: by holding the coin between the thumb and forefinger of my left hand, I pretended to grab it with my right, while allowing the coin to drop into the palm from which I'd appeared to have taken it. My son watched, eyes blinking lazily, then shrugged. "I knew that's how you did it," he said. Then he jerked the blankets over his head, and disappeared.

# HOLY HOURS

Patches the horse—who'd been taught how to answer the telephone, retrieve a beer from the refrigerator, ride in a convertible, and use his teeth to pull the covers of the bed he slept in over his shoulder—loved cheeseburgers. Maybe you know this already. Maybe you've seen the video where Patches' owner pulls up to a McDonald's drive-thru in a boatlike and possibly homemade white convertible splatted inexplicably with what looks like brown paint spots, and asks Patches, who's riding shotgun, if he wants a cheeseburger, and the horse nods and then sure enough, after the drive-thru lady hands over the food bag, the guy feeds Patches an honest-to-God cheeseburger. Thinking about Patches and how he learned to do all that he did and whether or not he might've cared had he known that those burgers he ate with such enthusiasm had been made out of the meat of fellow beasts of burden, made me think about Mister Ed, the talking horse. So I googled him. I learned that the actor Alan Young, who played Mister Ed's owner on the show, started the totally false rumor that trainers encouraged the horse who played Mister Ed—whose real name was Bamboo Harvester—to move his lips by putting peanut butter on his gums. This was maybe a better and more crowd-pleasing story than saying, "Though we used to put a nylon string in his mouth, he eventually learned how to move those lips on cue, simply by his trainer touching a finger to one of his hooves." In 1986, an Ohio preacher claimed that the "Mister Ed" theme song—you know, "a horse is a horse of course of course," etc.—contained a secret message and that if you played it backwards, listeners would hear the phrase "I sing this song for Satan." If you were a Christian teenager in the 1980s, as I was, you were no doubt disturbed—and also fascinated—by the idea that rock musicians might be secret Satan worshipers. You might have read *Rock's Hidden Persuader* or *Backward Masking Unmasked*, and you may have watched the documentary *Hell's Bells*, in which a man with a mustache and a mullet narrates the ways that the devil uses rock and pop and metal to turn humans away from God, and though a thirty-second section of this movie focused on The Cure, which was my favorite band at the time, it also seemed that the evidence against them was pretty weak, not only because the narrator claimed that "the unappealing nature of the church and Christianity is the subtle message of the song 'Faith,'" or because the documentary then featured a shot of the album cover overlaid with the lyrics "I cannot hold what you devour / the sacrifice of penance during the holy hour"—and not only because who could say for sure what "the holy hour" referred to, but also because the song seemed downright tame when compared to hits like "Blasphemous Rumors" by Depeche Mode, which claimed that God had "a sick sense of humor," or to "Dear God," a song by the band XTC in which the singer addresses the Almighty and says, "I can't believe in you." I was thinking about this documentary—and also about my boarding school's assistant chaplain, who'd engineered a Walkman so that it would play cassettes in reverse, so students could listen to "Stairway to Heaven" backwards and hear Robert Plant sing "my sweet Satan" in real time—when an alert appeared on my computer, an email from a former student named Angel, who happens to be spending the summer working at her aunt's real estate office in West Virginia, a state where, Angel claims, there are Trump signs everywhere, and she has to talk to clients who think Trump is some kind of savior, and that Obama is a terrorist, and that the people who deserve to be blamed for stuff are minorities and Millennials, both of which represent categories to which Angel belongs, and that she'd rather be at Virginia Beach, with her English bulldog, or in Atlanta, with her boyfriend, whom she once painted an eight-foot portrait of in a style that made him seem like some kind of baller gangsta saint—with a halo. Thunder boomed overhead. I welcomed it. I was at home by myself, safe in a house, supposedly writing, actually getting nostalgic about thirtysomething-year-old documentaries that purported to uncover the secrets of demon-inspired rock music when I realized that the windows in my car were down. I couldn't help, at this point, to miss my old neighbor and good friend Chris, who works at the Radford Arsenal, a plant that produces propellant for missiles used by the United States military, and who used to call me whenever it was starting to rain because he'd remember that he'd seen that I'd failed—once again—to raise my car windows, but now that we've moved across town, Chris cannot see my windows, and my new neighbors are either less observant or content to let me lie in whatever bed I make, which means that today I had to run outside, into a downpour so furious that it made the air brighter, as if the day had every intention of washing itself clean.

# BRING ME THE HEAD OF GERALDO RIVERA

My best friend's mom's boyfriend used to refer to G.I. Joe men as "dolls." "Hey," he'd say, "you guys playing with your little dolls again?" and though we'd try to argue that they should be referred to as "action figures," and that it was ludicrous to apply the word "doll" to a character like Serpentor, who, according to G.I. Joe comics, had been cloned with the help of Destro and Dr. Mindbender, who'd raided tombs the world over to harvest genetic material from history's most ruthless conquerors, so as to engineer the perfect Cobra leader, I worried that my best friend's mom's boyfriend might be right, that in the end our Joes were nothing but meaningless play pretties. On the occasions when my friend and I visited his mom's boyfriend's log cabin, we checked out the geodes arranged on a mantel, the dead flying squirrel in a freezer, and the picture of Jesus who, if you stared at him long enough, would suddenly open his eyes. We loved my best friend's mom's boyfriend's record collection, and spent afternoons flipping through his vinyl, listening to Andreas Vollenweider—a famous new age harpist—or studying the cover of The Beatles' *Sgt. Pepper's Lonely Hearts Club Band*. "Whoa," my best friend said, when the boyfriend pointed out Aleister Crowley, whose bald, pale head sat at the top of the left-hand crowd of people, between Sri Yukteswar (an Indian guru) and Mae West (famous Hollywood actress). We knew Aleister Crowley was trouble, that he was an English occultist, ceremonial magician, and drug addict, and that Led Zeppelin guitarist Jimmy Page had been so obsessed with him that he'd bought Crowley's house. I admit that recently, when I thought about the *Sgt. Pepper* album cover, the name that first came to mind was not Crowley but Anton LaVey, the author of *The Satanic Bible* and the founder of the Church of Satan. Crowley and LaVey look nothing alike; Crowley, at least in his later years, bears a resemblance to an avuncular British bureaucrat, whereas LaVey, with his goatee and shaved head—the result of a lost bet, and not, as he liked to claim, as a tribute to the tradition of ancient executioners—granted him a decidedly Mephistophilian appearance. If you were alive in the late 80s, you likely saw at least a portion of Geraldo Rivera's two-hour documentary "Exposing Satan's Underground," which was part talk show, part "investigative journalism," and whose "featured guests" included Zeena LaVey, a sultry-looking blond dressed in all black who happened to be Anton's daughter, and who had the distinction of having been, at age three, the first baptism performed by the Church of Satan. She and her partner Nikolas—a severe-looking dude with black hair, black clothes, and only one ear—had taken it upon themselves—in part because her father hadn't been interested—to defend the church, which had been targeted by the media as bearing responsibility for the supposed wave of abductions and ritual abuse slash sacrifices slash murders that had been purportedly committed in the name of Satan, whose literal existence, it's worth pointing out, LaVey and his church members didn't even believe in. Zeena and Nikolas would both eventually renounce Satanism and the occult, though their dedication to mysticism remains; they co-wrote a book about "sex magick," a series of ritualistic practices based on the idea that sexual energy can help people transcend the ways that they normally experience reality, and in 2002, they founded the Sethian Liberation Movement, which "allows people to learn and practice magic without answering to an oppressive sect and helps free ex-cult members from their troubled pasts." *Vice* magazine published an article by Zeena, in which she meditates on the subject of vice itself, and concludes by saying, "By resting in simply what is, instead of always trying to fix what is perceived as a defect, we open ourselves up to infinite possibilities." It—the article—is worth reading. I'll end this by saying that Zeena—in addition to all the other things she is—is also a musician, who's recorded a number of songs and albums, one of which, I am pleased to report, is titled "Bring Me the Head of Geraldo Rivera."

# WELL OF SOULS

My dad called to tell me that I shouldn't worry about running into deer on my bike; I should worry about running over a snake. Running over a snake, he explained, especially on a curve, would lay me out. My dad knows a lot about snakes; he lives with my mom in a house on property that borders National Forest, and before the house was built, when the land clearers arrived to cut and burn trees, they killed upwards of sixty copperheads and rattlesnakes. In the last quarter of a century, my parents have killed nearly a hundred. Often, when my father kills a venomous snake, he cuts off the head, peels the skin off like a banana from its body, which continues to writhe and jerk, then razors open its belly, to see what it's been eating—I've seen him pull out all kinds of things, and once watched as he unfurled the sopping wet tail of a squirrel. If he finds fetuses inside a dead snake, he counts those and adds them to that year's total killed-snake-tally. He's kept a few as pets before, in terrariums, on a screened-in porch—there's a picture somewhere of him blow-drying a frozen mouse to make it warm enough for the snake to be interested. Once, when moving a stack of logs on my parents' front porch, I decapitated, using the blade of a shovel, four copperheads. Regrettably, I also ended up killing a black snake who, before I identified him, was just another writhing body I had to contend with. My mother has video of me with a Ziploc bag of these snake heads; when I raise it to the camera, one of the heads

opens its mouth—like a yawn—and bears its fangs. I grew
up thinking that the serpent was the most beautiful creature
in the Garden of Eden, and that it had wings and could fly
through the air; in my head I pictured glittering ribbons
slithering through the air. Flying snakes—or Chrysope-
lea—don't really fly, but they can glide for long distances
by sucking in their stomachs, flattening their bodies, and
making continual serpentine motions, undulating laterally
from tree to tree. Remember the "Well of Souls" snake pit
scene in *Raiders of the Lost Ark*? Turns out, not all of those
snakes were snakes: some of them were legless lizards; others, pieces of rubber tubing. To generate the sound of thousands of snakes slithering around on top of each other, Ben
Burtt—a famous sound designer who used a scuba reg-
ulator to create Darth Vader's iconic respirations in *Star
Wars*—slid his fingers into a cheese casserole and rubbed
wet sponges against a skateboard's grip tape. To create the
whistling noises made by the spirits leaving the ark at the
end of the movie, Burtt ran the cries of various animals—
including humans, dolphins, and sea lions—run through
a vocoder, a device that was invented by a man named Homer Dudley, in part to help the United States communicate
its military secrets during World War II. Whenever I hear
the name Homer, it makes me think of the old mountain
man who lived not far from my father's office—an old man
who only had one ear and carried a buckeye in his pocket
for good luck, and once gave one of his doctors a toothpick,
then much later told him it had been carved from a raccoon's penis. I hadn't known this as a kid, but Homer also
carried, in his wallet, a bear vagina—an old, hairy piece of
leather that he'd bring out as a curiosity, a kind of conversation piece. Perhaps that's the same spirit that inspired my
father to use the United States Postal Service to send my

son the skin of a snake he'd recently killed. It arrived in an envelope, in a Ziploc bag. We opened it but it smelled bad and was greasy in a way that struck us as unpleasant, so we closed the bag tight. It stayed like that for a long time, until one day, when cleaning out a drawer, I came upon the skin again, and after thinking about how strange it was to have in my possession the outer covering of a creature that had once been alive—that had survived childhood, learned to hunt, hibernate, absorb sunlight, perhaps even mate—I admired the crossband pattern, and threw it—with little fanfare—into the garbage.

# OUT OF LIVES

Last night, I mistook the flashing button of a printer in the guest bedroom for lightning. Later, I heard a noise—as if something, somewhere, had been knocked over—so I grabbed the Mag-Lite on my bedside table and ventured out of the bedroom; when I clicked the light off and on to check on what might be in the bathroom, the bright white of the toilet startled me. What might I have done had I found an intruder? Used the flashlight as a club to shatter the burglar's skull? I don't own a gun, except for a tiny pistol that fires blanks—the kind used for signaling the starts of races, and which my grandmother gave to me years ago, for a reason I can no longer remember—and it's so old I'm afraid to pull the trigger, for fear—and I know this is stupid—that somehow it might explode in my hand. It's true that sometimes I go on shooting sprees in *Grand Theft Auto V*—I just start shooting whoever's around until the police arrive, and then I start shooting cops until I die—and that sometimes, in this game, I drive to the beach for the sole purpose of hunting people to run over, mowing down whole groups of beachgoers who've gathered around campfires, and that this—hearing them yell "oomph" and watching them flip into the air and over the car roof, in a slapsticky way—makes me laugh. Yes, these "people" bleed, but it's not fair, really, to say that they "die," not only because they were never alive to begin with, but also because after a minute or two their "bodies" disappear, and the only trace that they ever existed is a bloodstain and the money that popped out of their clothes when I hit them, and which glows a pulsing, radioactive green. I bought a headset so I could talk to other players when I play online, but now, every time I log on, it's either a foul-mouthed nine-year-old boy whose mother I can hear screaming one-sided conversations in the background or drawling adult men who aren't afraid to say the N-word or call each other "faggot." My son tells me that *Grand Theft Auto V* is a bad game, and when I ask him what he means, he says, "It's just bad!" The first time I remember being shamed for playing video games, I was riding down Main Street of my hometown in a truck with my father—past the A&P, past the drugstore, past the lunch counter where we'd order grilled cheese sandwiches with French fries and vanilla milkshakes—and out of nowhere, probably because I often felt a sense of camaraderie whenever I found myself riding alone with my father in his truck—I indulged an urge to confess a fantasy I'd just had—we'd passed an antique store and I had seen in its window shelves of glass vases and lamps—so I said, "Sometimes I think it would be fun to take an axe into a store where they sell a lot of glass stuff and chop it up." My father did not laugh. He did not say, "Yeah, smashing and breaking stuff can be fun sometimes" or "I can see how imagining such a thing could feel very liberating, perhaps even cathartic" or even "Ha ha, yeah, sounds fun but don't even think about it." Instead, without missing a beat, he said, "You play too many video games," a response that stunned me into silence, and which, upon reflection, I found disappointing, not only because it dismissed what I felt was a legitimately normal compulsion—who could in all honesty deny how much fun it would or could be to smash *stuff,* especially if said stuff happened to be highly shatterable—but also because it simply wasn't true: I didn't own an Atari or Intellivision console, didn't know many kids who owned them—didn't know many kids, period, because I lived in a small mountain town in the middle of nowhere and attended church school in a town twenty minutes away—and while it was true that I'd dropped a good number of quarters into the slots of the Kung-Fu Master and Spy Hunter cabinets at our local Video Den, it never took me long—fifteen minutes, tops—to burn through however much money I'd allotted for gameplay, mostly because my lack of experience resulted in what seemed to me to be ridiculously quick—and thus unfair—deaths. And yes, there was a mild amount of violence in these games: for instance, you had to time your punches and kicks just right in Kung-Fu Master or the goons would glom onto you and give you this weird group hug that would quickly diminish your health, and in Spy Hunter the whole point was to use the weaponry on G1655 Interceptor car (machine guns, smoke, oil slicks) to cause enemy cars to wreck and explode—but my all-time favorite game was Paperboy, the object of which, mundane as it might sound, was to deliver papers to subscribers without throwing them through windows, while avoiding obstacles like dogs, skateboarders, sidewalk breakdancers, mini-tornadoes, kids playing with remote control cars, and the Grim Reaper; in that game, you didn't even die when your turn was over—you were fired. I can't remember the first actual video game I ever played, but I can still remember the first time that somebody—a kid named Stirling—described Pac-Man to me: he'd asked if I'd ever heard of the game and I'd said no and so he said, "It's cool, you control a little guy who's being chased by ghosts and then when he eats a power pellet he gets to chase the ghosts and eat *them*." I found this description utterly confounding, in part because the phrase "little man who eats ghosts" made absolutely zero sense. And yet, the first time I played it—on a tabletop machine, in a Pizza Hut—it suddenly all came together. And the other day, when my son and I traveled to Roanoke, to visit a museum exhibit of upright arcade cabinet games, it was this same game I kept coming back to, the only one that made sense to play, in part because it allowed me to navigate a maze while being chased, and every time, to summon that old fear: a delightfully panicked state I inhabited whenever I was sure that something was gonna get me, but even if it did, I'd be okay—at least until I ran out of lives.

# LAND OF ENCHANTMENT

Four years have now passed—incidentally, the same amount of time it takes for light from Alpha Centauri, the nearest known star to the sun, to reach Earth—since I visited a New Mexican shaman. I chose New Mexico because I wanted to journey to someplace far away and magical and because New Mexico, which lives nearly two thousand miles from me, on the other side of the country, is known as the Land of Enchantment. I chose the shaman because she had a decent website and I liked the way she used her "About Me" page to tell the story of how, decades earlier, she had journeyed to Morocco to study with Paul Bowles and to Spain to receive the blessing of an older shaman, an old woman who recognized the younger as someone whom she could pass on the lineage of her teachings. I also liked the fact that she didn't look like a shaman—assuming it's safe to say that American shamans can be said to have a "look"—but instead appeared simply to be the kind of vibrant, radiantly happy middle-aged woman who could rock braids without it seeming like a superficial way to appear girlish. I rented a car from Virginia Tech's Fleet Services—a Prius whose license plate frame announced that the vehicle was "FOR OFFICAL USE ONLY"—and drove the 1600-plus miles to Santa Fe. In a room decorated with intricately woven rugs and Buddha statues and an ottoman where a plate of sage was smoldering, the shaman took a drum the size of a manhole and beat it while singing what sounded to me like an ancient, droning hymn. And when she entered the spirit realm or whatever—I know I'm messing this part up—she said she found my wisdom soul, an entity in the shape of a boy who, according to the shaman, had abandoned me when I was six years old; he now lived on a dude ranch in Wyoming, because the sky was so big out there and he loved the stars. Even so, this wisdom soul told the shaman that he wanted to "come home" and would I let him and if so would it be okay if he brought the stars too. I said yes and the shaman blew on the top of my head and then against my chest, as if she were blowing right into my heart; her breath smelled faintly—though not unpleasantly—of garlic. My job then, the shaman said, was to welcome the wisdom soul, to speak to it, to get to know it, and also to take a packet of tobacco she'd given me and sprinkle it around the base of a so-called "grandfather tree," as a thank you to ancestral spirits, or something, the latter of which I eventually did, but I have to admit that I never talked to the wisdom soul, didn't know how, really, or what I would say, never really believed that there ever even *was* an actual wisdom soul, though I wonder now if that was even the point—that instead I was supposed to learn to talk to a metaphorical part of myself I'd failed to nurture or even know. The day before I visited the shaman, I'd left the town of Marfa, Texas— where I'd spent the night in a vintage Airstream, and eaten chili poured into a bag of Fritos, and drank a margarita with jalapeños floating around inside—and driven north, to visit Prada Marfa. You may have heard of this place—a building that looks like a Prada store, in the middle of the desert. Even though the signs on the store say "Prada," and the letters exhibit the company's familiar font, and even though there are windows through which you can view various bags and shoes that appear to have been arranged on shelves in a manner that suggests that they might be for sale, they are not, because this store is not, as it turns out, an actual store. The door, for instance, is not a door that can be opened. The point of this thing, according to Elmgreen and Dragset, the pair of artists who designed it, was to build a monument to capitalism and then let nature take its ruinous course—and if somebody shot out a window or desert animals began to use it as a home, so be it—but days after it was finished, a thief broke in and stole everything inside. So the designers replaced the broken windows with fortified glass, cut the bottoms out of the bags, displayed only right-footed shoes, and tagged everything with GPS trackers. As much as I like to think about this fake little Prada store in the middle of the desert—the closest town, Valentine, has a population of 230—I think I would've liked it better if the creators had stayed true to their word. I like to imagine the building gradually falling apart, and that if somebody time-lapsed this decay, it might resemble something eaten by quicksand. As terrifying as the idea of falling into quicksand is, there is something pleasurable— to me, anyway—about watching something get sucked into the ground and out of sight. I hadn't ever given this phenomenon much thought, and I certainly wasn't aware that anyone would consider the sight of another person struggling and crying as they sank slowly into a bog or any kind of mushy earth to be arousing, but apparently this is a legit fetish and there are filmmakers whose entire oeuvre consists of other humans—usually women, in various stages of undress, but not, necessarily, naked—sinking slowly out of sight. I know, from reading several books on the subject, that if a person—a shaman, say, or someone under a shaman's direction—wants to travel from ordinary reality—that is, our everyday reality, with its limitations—to non-ordinary reality—that is, a spirit realm where *anything* is possible, where animals talk and people fly and our dead ancestors roam freely—that the traveler lies down on the floor, eyes closed, listens to the beat of a drum, and imagines climbing into a hole in the earth, and tunnels through the dark until light appears, and that this is one way to gain entrance to this so-called spirit realm, where, with one's power animal, one might seek the kind of wisdom that can make life in ordinary reality more bearable. I wonder, now, if quicksand could be seen as a kind of hole—a hole in disguise, like the booby traps I used to make by scooping out hollows at the edge of our yard and then laying twigs and leaves over the top—and that maybe a person could use quicksand as another way to journey to non-ordinary reality. I suppose it could be argued that quicksand isn't a hole, per se, but I seem to remember that the important thing was that one should imagine an entrance into the earth, and that this was an important part of exiting everyday reality. So who's to say in the end that I can't lie down, eyes closed, with the others who are listening to the beat of an ancient drum, to visit the jungle of my mind, where I'll shimmy myself into a patch of quicksand, and wait for the sopping muck to swallow me whole, so that I can finally leave this world—and its rules—behind.

# SIGNS OF THE TIMES

In the Kroger gas station, a man behind a wall of bullet-proof glass wearing a name tag that said "Mark" and then under his name "I Can Make Things Right" took my credit card, so as to charge me for a single 12-ounce sugar-free Red Bull I was buying, because—and I'm not afraid to admit it—I was feeling a little low, and Red Bull "gives you wings." I couldn't help but wonder if and to what extent Mark would go in order to remain true to his name tag's word, and if so, what that might entail: always providing exact change? refilling the squeegee buckets? exchanging a rancid pre-packaged pimento cheese on white for a non-rancid one? I wondered if Mark Who Can Make Things Right had read The Gospel of Mark, which the vast majority of religious scholars believe—for a number of reasons, including the fact that so much of its story reappears in both Matthew and Luke—is the most ancient of the gospels, and if so, whether or not he—that is, Mark Who Can Make Things Right—was familiar with the original ending, the one that appears in the oldest version of this particular Gospel, in which two women who visit the tomb of Jesus find it empty and, after having been addressed by a stranger who tells them that the Christ had risen, and that they should go tell his disciples, they run away from the tomb, and say nothing to anyone, because they're afraid, and then that's it, story's over, the end. If Mark Who Can Make Things Right isn't familiar with this shorter, older, and perhaps more authentic version of Mark, he no doubt had read the headline of today's *USA Today*—a stack of them were sitting in a metal cradle by the door—which claimed that Donald Trump's supporters were not clichés. I tried, as I exited, to think what that might mean, and why it was at all relevant, at least until I got distracted by a poster in the window of the Subway next door, which promised me that the chain's new buffalo chicken had been raised without antibiotics, a pronouncement I jeeringly slow-clapped to in my head. On the way to Radford, where I went to pick up my son and his friend from soccer camp, I found myself behind a car whose rear window was stickered with various messages: one, using individual letters, spelled out, simply and slightly wonkily, "Ted Cruz"; another implored me to "Never Forget Benghazi." I have to admit that I am not the type of person to glue signage to the back of my car (though my wife did once put an "OBAMA" sticker on the back of our Volvo, which the friend we sold it to clawed off with his fingernails after he broke down in the middle of West Virginia); I therefore have failed to identify myself to the other travelers on America's byways as a "Friend of Coal" or a person who hearts mountains, or as a person who thinks of himself as a Jesus Fish Person or Fish with Legs Person or a Fish With Legs Person Eating Fish People Person. The only bumper sticker I can think of that I'd be interested in is one that I could place over that one that says "Never Forget Benghazi," but I have a feeling that "Never Forget How the Bush Administration Ignored Warnings about 9/11 and Then Based on Faulty Evidence If Not Outright Lies Waged a War with Another Country that Killed by Lowest Estimate 150,000 Lives and Highest Estimate Over a Million and Then Failed to Meet the Needs of Its 32,226 Wounded Soldiers, Not to Mention the Countless

Other Veterans Who Returned with Serious Post-Traumatic Stress Syndrome, Many of Whom Committed Suicide, So If You're More Concerned with the Four American Lives Lost in Benghazi Than that Other Mindblowingly Farcial Fiasco I Have No Other Choice But to Hereby Christen You 'A Piece of Human Garbage'" probably wouldn't fit on a bumper sticker, at least not one big enough to read. Still, I'd like to get some made. I would've given one to the guy I saw at a local bar—The Underground—the other night, an older black man in a ball cap who asked me how I was doing and when I said, "Pretty good and you," replied with, "I'm alive and breathing, and if that's the case I got no complaints," then proceeded to tell me that, years ago, he'd been in Iraq—the Gulf War, I guessed, but didn't ask—and that he said he'd done everything he was asked to do, because that's how you survived that shit, you shot men, women, and even children if you had to, because over there, children weren't just children, they were small humans who may or may not have clay bombs strapped to their chests. "I did what I had to do," he said. "And I didn't think twice about it," he added. "And now here I am." He lifted a tumbler of ice and pale green liquid to his face. "I guess you had to learn how to be a machine," I said, but if the man heard me, he didn't reply. His eyes were glazed over, and before he turned to go away, he held up two fingers, and said he hoped I had a blessed day.

# STAY WOKE

Last night at the Clifton Inn in Charlottesville, Virginia—specifically, in the Meriwether Lewis room, whose bathroom shower is made of the kind of flagstone rock you often find on fireplace mantels, and where I was spending some QT with the wife while our son spent the week at summer camp—I woke to the sound of rustling and thought: *mouse.* I checked my phone. 3:15 a.m. Outside, I knew, it was 83 degrees, but we'd set the inside temperature to 64, so we could comfortably burrow under our covers. I burrowed under the covers. Earlier, my wife had informed me that corn sweat in Iowa was a contributing factor to the heat dome, which we were able to escape, the day before, by floating in the Inn's waterfall infinity pool. In Roanoke, where the heat index surpassed 105, Donald Trump spent a good portion of his speech berating the operators of the hotel where he was speaking and said that "the ballroom (sic) . . . should be ashamed." According to a headline on Facebook, the temperature in Iran had reached 129 degrees. I didn't like to think about the slow but steady warming of the earth—of dissolving icebergs or rising seas or the melting glacier in Switzerland whose glowing blue caverns I'd explored as a teenager—so, in my head, I replayed the things I'd seen during the previous day's trip to a series of stores that specialized in selling discarded artifacts: obsolete televisions, creepy dolls, a box of keychains, an acoustic guitar emblazoned with images of rose petals, a collection of laserdiscs, a mask of a political figure whose identity I couldn't confirm. At one point, when I'd picked up an old popcorn popping contraption, eyeballed the price tag, and indignantly shouted out the number, my wife shushed me, and explained that nobody bought stuff like that to actually use; they bought stuff like that because it was old and authentic and they wanted to hang it on a wall. I picked up a pair of salt shakers—one resembled an African-American butler, the other a stereotypical Mammy—and thought about the statue on my grandmother's kitchen windowsill, the one that depicts a little black boy in overalls, carrying a burlap sack filled with cotton, and then I wondered what Lorraine, the African-American woman who takes care of my 97-year-old grandmother, thinks when she sees it, and what she would've thought about the painting that someone in my family gave my wife and me years ago at our baby shower, which depicted a black woman wearing a headscarf and nursing a white baby—a painting that, I believe, we soon after threw into the garbage. I heard the rustling again, used my phone to shine a light across the room. I imagined the mouse working its way through the maze of snacks my wife and I had bought the night before at a gourmet grocery store, from a cashier—a friendly black woman—who agreed that yes, it was okay to splurge on vacation, she did the same thing. My wife, who is a very light sleeper, woke, asked what it was. "A mouse, maybe," I said. "Turn on the light," she said. I turned on the light. Something the size of a thumb darted along the fireplace tile. "I saw it," I said. I gathered the snacks we'd left sitting on the fireplace hearth—chili-flavored popcorn, banana pepper-flavored potato chips, and dark chocolate-covered salted caramels—and placed them into a paper sack. I placed the sack on top of a chest of drawers, next to a complimentary carafe of Madeira, which, I knew, because I'd read the accompanying laminated sheet of paper, was a fortified wine from a volcanic island 400 miles off the coast of Morocco, and was the same wine with which the Declaration of Independence had been toasted. I flicked off the light. The rustling sounded again. I wondered what to do if I actually found the mouse; although I had considered flattening it to a bloody pulp with a fireplace tool—specifically the little shovel—I wasn't sure I had the stomach for it. I remembered the bag of popcorn that we'd stuffed into a plastic-lined basket in the bathroom. I could see the little mouse in my mind; she was holding a kernel of popcorn with both claws, turning it over and over as she nibbled it down to a nub. I got up, threw a towel over the trash can, opened the door, and set it outside. I couldn't lock the door—for some reason, it wouldn't shut flush enough with the frame to allow the bolt to slide into the gap in the strike plate. I gave up, returned to bed. To distract myself from the thought of bad men kicking open the door and shooting us in our sleep, I composed, in my head, a reply to a former student, whose email I had received the day before but hadn't yet responded to. This particular student had written to inform me that she might be in need of a recommendation, but she also wanted to know whether I ever had days when I felt completely lonely and heartsick when I realized that someday we would all die, like every living thing and there would be nothing more forever? I remembered then something I'd read that Alan Watts had written, something along the lines of "you don't remember your birth, and you won't remember your death," so commit to live in the place you'll never leave—i.e., the present, and told myself not to forget that when I woke the next morning. I closed my eyes and remembered, as I often do when I can't sleep, how a dear friend had once told me that when he couldn't sleep he just surrendered to the idea that he wouldn't, and told himself that keeping his eyes closed and just resting was the next best thing. I can't remember if I heard the mouse again—only that as I let go of what to think of next, the dreams began to come.

# TRICK-OR-TREAT

A fawn crossed the road as I began my descent—via bicycle—into the valley; I thought I could see little buds on its head, but I didn't trust that it was possible for a baby deer to have horns of any kind. At the bottom of the valley, in a field, hundreds of spider webs—spread vertically between grass blades, billowing slightly in wind—glistened so mesmerizingly that it seemed as if their sole purpose was decorative: a net upon which droplets of dew had been strewn like jewels, for maximum enjoyment of light refraction. Still, I couldn't get the horns out of my head: they called to mind the tiny devil figurine that sits on the windowsill above my kitchen sink, and which once sat on the windowsill above the kitchen sink in the house where I grew up during the month of October, along with a tiny scarecrow, jack-o'-lantern, and witch. I've always liked devils when depicted cutely as cartoonish imps, and once bought my two-year-old son a red costume that had a hood with little black horns emerging from each side. I thought: my wife will be forty this year on Halloween, maybe I should do something like contact all her high school and college friends and get them to write memories about her, but then I remembered: she already turned forty—*two years ago*. Yesterday, at Kroger, I noticed a whole line of Halloween figures—pumpkins and ghosts—outside on the sidewalk and heard somebody else say what I was thinking, and what probably corporate execs or whoever's idea it was to set them out so early had also thought, which was: "Halloween stuff? It's not even August yet." A couple days before, my six-year-old nephew held up a trick-or-treat bucket in the shape of Darth Vader's head he'd found in our storage room and gasped. "You guys trick-or-treat?" he said. "Sure," I said. "And you dress up?" he asked. "Yes," I said. His brow was furrowed, his eyes wide. "That's the bad part," he whispered. I told my sister this and she said, "Yeah, we don't do trick-or-treating." When I expressed disbelief, and reminded her that we had trick-or-treated as kids, she said that she knew that but they didn't, she didn't like ghosts or witches or any of that stuff. I didn't say ghosts or witches were like the two most boring things you could be, and that today's pop-up Halloween stores, though they had their share of gore, offered all sorts of alternatives to the occult and undead. So it was funny then, if only to me, to discover that "The Phantom" was the name of the brand of my sister's husband's drone, a four-bladed "quadcopter," which, according to its website, has a magnesium skeleton. I cheered when my brother-in-law flew The Phantom over the gate at the top of the golf course hill, the one that has a sign that says, "Absolutely NO Trespassing" and guards a vista of rolling hills and blue mountains, as I'd been meaning to jump that fence for a while, just to see what, according to the sign, I absolutely shouldn't experience. As it turns out, insuring privacy and maintaining boundaries are recurrent themes in the world where I live; all along Catawba Road, which winds through a long valley, beside a quiet stream where, last week, a particular ripple-shape made me imagine a crocodile swimming upstream, landowners have nailed signs to trees and fence posts that say "No Trespassing" or "No Hunting or Fishing or Trespassing Under Any Circumstances, Violators Will Be Prosecuted," and as far as I can tell, people tend to obey, because for as many years as I've passed these fields, which are home to cows and sometimes deer, I've almost never seen an actual human being in any of them, ever. Humans, for the most part, stick to the road, which is twisty and narrow and traveled by drivers who know it so well that they travel at unnerving speeds. I used to be afraid of riding on this road for that very reason; though I'm not anymore—not really—I often imagine, when I hear an approaching engine, that a bumper will clip my back wheel, and send me into a roadside ditch, where, nestled in long grass and among the Queen Anne's lace there seems every twenty-five yards or so to be some kind of discarded container: beer cans, McDonald's fry boxes, clamshell take-out boxes, and—don't ask me to explain—a preponderance of Bojangles' cups. The word "Bojangles'" always makes me think of Mr. Bojangles—not the song inspired by a homeless drunk in a New Orleans prison and not Bill "Bojangles" Robinson, who, as an actor and dancer, became the most recognized and wealthiest African-American entertainer in the first part of the 20th century, but a fictional man that my Uncle Ricky often referred to when I was a kid, the one he was always explaining had just disappeared whenever I turned to see who it was he was waving to, and who, according to my uncle, lived under a creek bank in a place on my grandparents' property referred to as "The Bottoms," where he kept a gunny sack full of kids he'd stolen and planned to eat. I never really believed in Mr. Bojangles, but it was fun to pretend, especially if it involved my aunt Mary Jane, who happened to be Uncle Ricky's wife—a pretty, blond woman with blue eyes and babydoll eyelashes who laughed at her own jokes and carried a purse full of candy and expressed a kind of self-effacing incredulity if you admitted you hadn't watched *Felicity* or *Girls*, or if you hadn't heard of charm bracelets. In Mary Jane's world, it was a crime not to leave cookies for Santa on Christmas Eve, and dolls came to life at night when people were sleeping and roamed around their houses, and the sound of thunder signaled a retreat to a special closet in her house, where she kept games and snacks and flashlights especially for this exact occasion: a storm. When I was little, she led me through the pine forest that separated my grandparents' house from its surrounding neighborhood; I was Hansel, she was Gretel, and instead of breadcrumbs, we dropped M&M's on the trail, so we could find our way back. A few months ago, representatives from the Strange Bros.—South Carolina's premiere site development contractors—arrived, and cut down all the trees; they had been falling on the road and threatening surrounding homes. Mary Jane texted me pictures and video of the felled trees and a week later, in the mail, I received a padded envelope; inside, there was a plastic baggy of jagged, matchstick-sized shards of wood, labeled "The Pines." Mary Jane told me that the land would be replanted, but it would never be the same. What I wanted to tell her, but didn't: nothing ever is.

# NIGHT THOUGHTS

According to a DJ on K92, Justin Bieber—a Canadian pop star and heartthrob who's afraid of elevators and clowns and who once got an F in school but changed it by drawing two additional curves on the letter to a B so he wouldn't get in trouble—is taking a much-needed vacation in Hawaii, where he'll stay at Water Falling Estate: a mansion that sits at the edge of a promontory overlooking the Pacific. For $10,000 a night, you too can enjoy the amenities of Water Falling Estate, which includes a rooftop helipad, a central Daytona 52-inch round pneumatic air-compression elevator that allows access to all floors of the main house, a basketball slash tennis court with stadium style seating for 450 spectators, and a trail leading to a naturally-occurring, three-tiered waterfall. According to The Pinnacle List, which markets luxury real estate to affluent buyers and is likely correct in assuming that its potential customers prefer residences that "evoke an unforgettable experience of living life beyond the limits of ordinary luxury expectations," Water Falling Estate is available for purchase at the cost of 18.2 million dollars. I know this because—using the World Wide Web—I looked inside of it. Its interior appears to be made of mahogany and marble and looks a little as if it had originally been designed as the World's Largest Funeral Home. Nothing about the phrase "Service Corporation International" suggests that it is—and it is—the world's largest funeral home and cemetery conglomerate, which may be the reason it operates under the name "Dignity Memorial." According to an article titled "Ten Companies That Control the Death Industry," death in America generates over 15 billion dollars in revenue a year for companies that supply bereaved humans with flowers, stones, plaques, caskets, urns, crypts, and funeral home equipment. Though you may be familiar with the concept of "embalming a corpse," did you know that the fluids drained from bodies are likely to enter your local public sewage systems? Grief management pioneer Erich Lindemann argued that bereavement can become complicated for those who never had the opportunity to view the body of a dead person they loved; this may have something to do with our country's longstanding, if highly invasive, insistence on corpse preservation. As effective as modern-day embalming practices are in ensuring that cadavers remain "lifelike," bodies filled with formaldehyde will—like those preserved by ancient Egyptians, who believed souls would return to adequately preserved bodies—eventually deteriorate. The best and most environmentally responsible option for the disposal of dead bodies might involve alkaline hydrosis, during which the deceased is placed into a chamber of water and lye, and heated at a high pressure to 160 degrees—a process that results in green-brown liquid and porous, easily crushable bone fragments. The fluid is then discarded, and the remains pulverized using a Cremulator, a machine invented by a company called DFW Europe, one that separates ferro- and non-ferrometals (that is, metals that contain appreciable amounts of iron and those that do not) while automatically filling an urn with the resultant "ash." The home page of DFW Europe—which, as you might guess, has nothing to do with David Foster Wallace, the bandana-wearing, tobacco-chewing author of intellectually challenging literary fiction, who committed suicide by hanging himself from a patio rafter—features a photo of a series of three cremation furnaces: chunky, symmetrical, stylized blocks that look as if they might've been designed by avant-garde German architects; into one of these furnace chambers, an ivory casket appears to be in the process of entering the red-hot mouth of an incinerator. Humans are rarely pictured on DFW's site, and when they do appear they look friendly and pleasantly engaged, as do the people on the company's "Training Course" page, who are wearing all black and enjoying tea while learning about the theory and practice of operating a cremation furnace, during which time the presenters will explore "the question of what exactly is meant by a calamity and how to deal with it responsibly." I can't be the only person on earth who hears the word "calamity" and thinks immediately of Calamity Jane, the American frontierswoman whose vices, according to one of her friends, "were the wide-open sins of a wide-open country—the sort that never carried a hurt." Jane may not have been quite as daring as she claimed, and her exploits likely did not include the shooting of Indians; nonetheless, she made appearances in so-called "dime museums" across the United States. In 1892, Kohl & Middleton's Globe Dime Museum, in which Calamity Jane was once featured, ran an advertisement in the Chicago Tribune that announced: FIRST TIME ON PUBLIC EXHIBITION, 6 PEOPLE TURNING TO STONE, LIVING PETRIFIED, FAMILY FROM IDAHO, THE GRANDFATHER OF THIS REMARKABLE FAMILY IS A SOLID MAN TURNED TO ROCK, HE HAS NOT BREATHED FOR 20 YEARS, SLUMBERING WITH THE GREAT MAJORITY. This beguiling caption was accompanied by a somewhat primitive cartoon of a group of smiling figures who appeared to be unable to bend their knees or elbows. If "slumbering with the great majority" rings at all familiar to your ears, it may have something to do with a section of a nine-part poem by Edward Young titled, "Night-Thoughts," which includes the following observation: "Life is the desert, life the solitude; / Death joins us to the great majority." Such words might prove comforting to those who fear the unknown: everyone who has ever lived has emerged from it; to it everyone will return. Most of us, however, will remain, as ever, somewhat troubled—if not downright afraid—by the thought of our eventual demise, and because we will continue to seek solace where we can find it, we will be grateful when we turn on our radios and hear one of our country's beloved pop stars crooning his most current hit, a tune that came to him on one of those nights when, after taking a single hit from a water pipe—a lungful of Jack Flash his bodyguard scored at a Denver marijuana dispensary, and which The Cannabist had described as "astounding in every way . . . flavor, yield and mind-body potency are virtually unparalleled"—the young man swam to the edge of Water Falling Estate's 25-meter Olympic-size infinity pool, noted the sound of distant waves crashing on the rocks below and the moonlight glimmering like a thousand knife blades upon the Pacific, said a prayer for all the blessings of his improbable—if admittedly ephemeral—existence, and began—without thinking too much or even at all about where he was going—to sing.

# HANDS UP

It was too hot to cycle—according to the weather app on my phone, the humidity topped out at 100%—but I suited up anyway, filled my bike tires, climbed aboard, clicked shoes into pedals, and glided away. I'd spent the morning walking to and from the Blacksburg Farmer's Market, where the dog and I had met my wife after her Saturday morning run, and where we bought tomatoes and green beans and Thai basil and two frozen chicken breasts vacuum-sealed in plastic but no beef because our regular provider—a little dude with an overbite and a goatee and ratty baseball cap who wears the same *Fahrenheit 451* T-shirt every week and always takes the time to inform interested customers that cooking a steak should begin with "a NASA-hot grill"—wasn't there, so we left, walking up Roanoke Street, past a series of not-yet-opened vendor tents lining the sidewalks for our town's annual street festival, whose vendors included purveyors of homemade dog treats, photorealistic paintings of Appalachian landscapes, hand-forged metal items, candles, jewelry, and various permutation of meats on sticks. I peeled an orange "Guns Save Lives" sticker from a telephone pole, crumpled it in my fist, tossed it into a flowerbed, and thought of what I might say to the guy at the "Guns Save Lives" tent who stands there all day—Glock holstered proudly to his belt—handing out stickers to anyone who'll take them, many of whom press them, as if pledging allegiance, over their hearts. I wanted to point out that, as catchy a slogan as "Guns Save Lives" might be, there were probably a great many other things in the world that were far better at saving lives, like doctors, CPR, defibrillators, bed rest, seatbelts, a Mediterranean diet, a steady hand, clean water, blankets, medicine, flare guns, and love. I crested one of our town's tallest hills, bracing myself for the long, fast descent into the valley, during which I dreamed about somehow having the road entirely to myself, or at least renting a ten mile or so strip of it for an hour so I could safely wear headphones, as this might help me kill the two-headed, week-long earworm that had been living in my head, and which repeated—with a relentless urgency—either the name "Lakshmi Singh" or the chorus from "Hands Up" by the band Blood Orange. Lakshmi Singh is a reporter from National Public Radio; the name Lakshmi is the name of the Hindu goddess of wealth and prosperity. "Hands up, get out" is what police officers often shout at suspects they want to surrender; however, in the wake of recent deaths of young black men who have been shot by police officers, the phrase has become a rallying cry for protesters. Dev Hynes is the name of the person—a young black man from England—behind Blood Orange, and on the day his latest album dropped, and on which the song "Hands Up" appears, he dedicated the music—a collection of groovy, falsetto-powered R&B numbers—to anyone who'd been told that they were "not black enough, too black, too queer, not queer the right way." I hoped the music could be for me, too, a person who not only wanted to understand what all that might mean, but also to get outside himself, who often took long bike rides on a dangerous two-lane road because it led out of the town where he lived, past an imposing mountain that today— what with a gray cloud hovering over its summit—looked vaguely volcanic, not because he had some kind of death

wish but simply so that he could escape the banalities of
his life for an hour and so that he could say hi to the little
church whose sign said "ALL ARE WELCOME," and hi
to the faded metal placard hanging from a pole on the side
of a barn that said, "PET Pasteurized Milk" and hi to the
cows knee deep in the creek, whose swishing tails called to
mind the beasts' moist, fly-bombarded orifices, and how
the patient blinking of their long-lashed eyelids seemed
like an embodiment of what it meant to be long-suffering.
My own eyes felt beleaguered: I kept trying and failing to
wipe away sweat but my gloves were sopping, so I stopped
to scoop creek water onto my face. Though I was eager to
get home and stand under an air conditioning vent and
get blasted by a cold metallic breeze, I stopped once more,
to inspect an orange newt whose head had been crushed
into the asphalt. I took a picture of this little guy, and after posting it to Instagram with the tag "#exoticroadkill,"
I remembered the video I'd shot on the way to the ATM
this morning, before I met my wife at the farmer's market,
the one that featured a just-hatched cicada on its back—
centimeters from the brittle exoskeleton (or "nymph skin")
from which it had emerged—pedaling its legs helplessly. I'd
videoed myself flipping over the bug, and had planned to
post this to Instagram as well, to give the world a glimpse
of my largesse slash magnanimity, but then I discovered
that the cicada's left wing had been folded backwards and
didn't appear to be functional. Although I hoped that the
wing might right itself, I didn't stay to find out, and in the
end, I posted a shot of the insect—its tapered body as iri-
descent as a baby leaf in spring—exactly as I had found it:
spinning its legs in vain.

# SINKHOLE

You're not supposed to look at your phone first thing in the morning, at least that's what an article I read recently—on my phone—told me, but I always wake up wondering what happened in the world while I was sleeping, so that's exactly what, every morning, I do. Today, I scrolled through my feed—bypassing links to articles about Trump's call to have Hillary assassinated and "Alfred Hitchcock's Literary Legacy" and all those female runners who somebody keeps murdering—I paused, and let one of those "watch from above as food is prepared" videos play, specifically a so-called "one-pot" recipe for spaghetti, a dish that, in the end, didn't look very appealing. I resolved to make spaghetti myself, and I resolved to make it in a far superior manner, using San Marzano tomatoes, garlic, basil, butter, and—for the meatballs—ground buffalo meat, panko breadcrumbs, and ricotta cheese. You may have heard that buffalo meat is lower in cholesterol and thus better for the heart than beef, but it's still a red meat, too much of which, I know, has been linked to heart attacks, and these, so I've come to understand, are more deadly in middle-aged men; often, when I'm pedaling up a very long, steeply-graded hill, I imagine my heart exploding: I know that's not what happens during a heart attack but because of how hard it's pounding it sort of feels like it might. I've often thought that if a study came out determining that cycling was bad for one's health, I would still do it, not only because it allows me to burn enough calories so that I can pretty much eat and drink as much as I want and still retain a figure that resembles a svelte pear, but because it's fun and it makes me feel afterwards—and I suppose this is true—as if both my mind and my body have been detoxified. A former student asked me recently if my bike route was dangerous and I told him that even though it can be a little unnerving to have a dual cab Ford pickup blast by you at 50 mph, my sense was that however obnoxious drivers can be—I always imagine that they are miffed when they come upon a cyclist—they would rather not murder me, even if I am wearing funny clothes. I think about crashing every time I go out—and thanks to the spectacular wreck of that female Dutch cyclist at the Olympics, I have a very particular image to summon: the back wheel rising, the body flying headfirst over handlebars—but I spend most of my time during my rides as a receptacle for awe and wonder, noting, say, a skink ribboning across the pavement, or the webbed mesh of a leaf in the road that at first tricks me into thinking it's the wing of a butterfly, or the dazzling actual wings of a butterfly as it sucks vital minerals from a pile of excrement. I might think a thought like I thought today, a thought like: If somebody told me I was going to die tomorrow, next week, or next month, I wouldn't be happy about it, but I also couldn't argue—not in the least—that I hadn't lived a full life. Halfway through today's ride, I found a children's book titled *Stanley the Farmer*, whose cover featured a cartoon hamster riding a tractor, sitting in the middle of the road, so I picked it up and—savoring the completion of an anonymous good deed—placed it on a fence post in front of a nearby house, not knowing whether anyone there had checked out the book, or if it had been shoved by tiny hands out the window of a passing car; either way, I hoped it might find its way back to the Montgomery County Library, whose name had appeared on a label stickered to its spine. Of course, I can't see the name "Stanley" and not think of Stanley the dog, a yellow lab who was supposed to die of cancer years ago, and whose owners—my very good friends—fed him a steady diet of bacon and steak, and even took him on a trip to the beach, thinking that because doctors had given him no more than three months to live, he deserved to retrieve a few tennis balls from the ocean, but that was three years ago, and Stanley's as fine a dog as ever, barking ferociously at me every time I come to the door, and patiently waiting, until I utter the word "Okay," to gobble the piece of cheese I've placed on his paw; once, when my friend Katy did this trick, she forgot to say "Okay," and so Stanley waited and waited and finally picked up the treat with his mouth and carried it into a room and placed it on the floor before his owner, who felt badly that she'd made him wait but was—as she should have been—impressed at what a very good boy he had been. Stanley would love to swim in the creek that winds alongside Dry Run Road, a narrow strip of gravel I ride to get from Catawba Road to Mt. Tabor Road; today was the first day all summer I'd seen it flush with water; in fact, the stream flowed so lavishly, so abundantly, it would've been hard to imagine that only days before it'd been a trough of dusty rocks. This phenomenon—that of a disappearing and reappearing creek—was explained to me by another cyclist—a mechanical engineer, who'd startled me when, the week before, during another ride on this same road, he'd come up behind me and said, simply, "Hi"—who surmised that the creek's fluctuations were the result of a sinkhole, which can suck up only so much water: if there's more than it can drink, the creek keeps going; if not, it peters out. I passed the little white clapboard house where only once did I ever see a little man sitting on his porch, who waved when I waved, but I didn't wave to the little blond girl, the one who was setting a bowl of water down in the grass for two white pups, because I didn't know her and didn't want to put her in the position of having to wave to a stranger. And, on this day, I did sort of feel like an alien on an exploratory mission; it occurred to me, as I glided closer toward town, that the day was so vivid—*so real*, I caught myself thinking. Too many video games? For the first time yesterday, on my son's first day of eighth grade, I played *No Man's Sky*—a game about survival and space exploration that, thanks to a computer algorithm, creates itself as you play it, and which, according to the little guy at GameStop, would take every person on earth playing it continuously for sixty years to explore the game in its entirety; as soon as my son got home he laid out a series of papers the school needed me to sign, but I was too busy exploring a cave on a virtual planet, trying and failing to find enough resources to repair my spaceship. I learned too late that every time I died—thanks to a spider-like bug that kept attacking me—I needed to return to the site of my death, since if I visited the grave of my previous self, I could recover the resources I'd left behind when I died. I chided myself for wasting so much time in a virtual world, and the thought occurred to me that I am no more magnanimous than when I am riding my bike: High on an endorphin-blast, my brain surges, and whatever sinkhole normally sucks up my gratefulness for being alive is flooded with said gratefulness, causing me to acknowledge that I've done nothing to earn a life as good as the one I have, where I can spend the entire summer—when I'm not mowing the lawn or washing dishes or cooking dinner or responding to email or walking the dog—riding my bike and reading books and writing, and that I love my house and town and family, and thereby pledge forevermore to be kinder to everyone, but then, once my ride's over and I've showered and snacked and am driving my kid to soccer practice, I'm back to my old egocentric self, exasperated by my son's inquisitive cheerfulness, because it's distracting me from the news story Audie Cornish is introducing on NPR, or annoyed by the fact that my wife—who has the metabolism of a hummingbird—is crunching another dill pickle chip while I'm trying to think, which means that I have no choice but to confess that the best version of myself—because it lives only in my imagination and is thus virtual—has yet to see the light of day.

# SPOILER ALERT

I can't stop recommending Truman Capote's *Music for Chameleons*, and when I do, I always provide the following three examples to illustrate the treasure trove of oddities lurking within its pages: 1., a couple who, not long after receiving a miniature hand-carved coffin with their picture inside, climbed into their car, where they were repeatedly bitten by nine giant rattlesnakes that had been injected with amphetamines; 2., a whorehouse in New Orleans that served cherries—cooked in cream and absinthe—from an octoroon's vagina; and 3., a movie star who once played "You Are My Sunshine" on a piano using not his hands, but his penis. These were, according to Capote, real things that happened. Another real thing that happened: I attended a meeting with my department chair and a woman whose research examines the attempts to preempt and eradicate biological danger; together, we brainstormed activities for an event called "Viral Imaginations," one that would include a reading and craft talk by author Justin Cronin, who wrote a series of very long books that I will never read about a vampire apocalypse triggered inadvertently by military scientists, who inject twelve subjects with an experimental drug made from a virus taken from a South American bat, which grants, to the infected, psychic powers and a thirst for blood. Far more interesting than vampires, though, was the description the women provided about real-life guinea worms, a nematode parasite that can gain entrance to your body if you should ever drink water containing water fleas, who themselves have been infected with guinea worm larvae; a *year* later, after the larvae attach themselves to your intestinal wall, where they mate, the male dies and is reabsorbed into your body, while the female migrates through subcutaneous tissues and begins to emerge through your skin, the effect of which causes a blister and, I'd have no choice but to suppose, a great deal of distress, once you realize that a tiny worm is burrowing very slowly—it can take as long as several weeks—out of the flesh of your arm or your leg. "You should YouTube zombie insects," the expert on biological danger told me, and though I haven't yet, I probably soon will, though I doubt I will binge on those videos as voraciously as I did *Stranger Things*—a Netflix series about the disappearance of a boy in a small town and the appearance of a girl with supernatural powers who escaped from a government industrial complex, and who might be responsible for opening a portal between our universe and another, thus giving birth to a hideous *Alien*-like monster. The teenage girl who tried to shoot the monster—a bipedal thing whose body appeared to be covered in scales secreting slime and a head that opened up like a carnivorous flower— reminded me, when her forehead wrinkled with worry, of an ex-girlfriend of mine who, with her brother, had been killed instantly when an eighteen-wheeler rear-ended them after it had failed to slow for traffic produced by late night highway construction; at the funeral home, I peered into their caskets to say goodbye, and noted that they looked, what with their shining hair and purplish, sparkly makeup caking their faces, like a pair of storybook siblings who had drowned, but might, at any moment, be revived. I recently downloaded the soundtrack to *Stranger Things* and because the music is mostly keyboard washes and looped arpeggios, it has the power to inject otherwise ordinary events with import, making, for instance, a single green turd floating in the yellow water of a toilet bowl easier to imagine as a display of some hovering varietal of space rock that's able to grow its own golden aura. I figured that this perceptual shift might also be blamed on having played *No Man's Sky* on PlayStation yesterday; I wandered a virtual planet shooting various flora and fauna with a mining ray-gun, and observed a giant, turd-shaped rock floating inexplicably above a mountain that swished greenly with virtual grass. After coming home from church, where I read aloud to the congregation a passage from Hebrews in which the writer says that he doesn't have time to tell all the important faith stories from scripture, which include those "who through faith conquered kingdoms, administered justice, obtained promises, shut the mouths of lions, quenched raging fire, escaped the edge of the sword, won strength out of weakness, became mighty in war, put foreign armies to flight . . . were stoned to death, they were sawn in two, they were killed by the sword; they went about in skins of sheep and goats, destitute, persecuted, tormented, wandered in deserts and mountains, and in caves and holes in the ground," I noted that though I had mowed my lawn only three days before, the grass was nearly tall enough to warrant being cut again. I remembered that the couple who recently moved to our neighborhood had claimed that it was so hot and dry in Colorado that keeping a green lawn alive for a month required more water than an entire household would use during that same period of time. It's easy to forget that lawns, like so much of what we live with, are rather arbitrary conventions invented by man; in the Jacobean era of the early 17th century, lawns were a sign of wealth and status, and proved that their owners were wealthy enough to possess property that wasn't being used for animal grazing. And while having a yard of one's own can certainly feel luxurious, especially when walking barefoot over just-mown grass, I'm willing to bet that neither Hillary Clinton nor Donald Trump has ever mowed a lawn, much less tried to fit a mower into the back of a Honda CRV, so as to transport it across town for repairs, which is what I did over two weeks ago. Once the mower's fuel intake system has been rebuilt, I will fork over a sizeable amount of money for its release, and the man I pay, I know, from having paid him before, will have no left hand, merely a stump where a hand had once been, and I will wonder, as I always do, whether repairing machines with dangerous whirring metal blades is his way of proving to the universe that he's mastered the very thing that disfigured him—and that having successfully done so, he now has nothing to fear.

# OBSERVATORIUM

Years ago, I taught a class in a room that clearly had not been designed to be used as a classroom. I know this because it was barely large enough to hold fifteen desks and also because there was a window through which we could view the class next door, a class that was perhaps three times as large as our own. "Wait," one of my students—a young woman—said, on the first day of class. "Can they see us?" I assured her that they could not; I'd visited the other classroom—the one we could see—and knew that if you looked at the window from the other side, you would see your own reflection, nothing more, no matter how close you got to the mirror. Every day, we arrived at this tiny classroom and did our best to arrange the desks in a circle—actually, it was more of an oblong rectangle—so that students could see each other as they discussed the stories that they'd written and brought to class to politely nitpick to death, but also to give the impression that while I might be the teacher of record, I was more of a leader, and that all voices and opinions mattered equally. Little attention was given to the window, though I'd often catch students absentmindedly staring at the next class during workshops, and I too might sneak a glance or two after having assigned an in-class writing prompt. One day, as an exercise in observation, and because the window was there and I figured it ought to be put to use, I asked my students to leave their notebooks on their desks and gather at its edge. "What exactly do you want us to do?"

one student said. "Just watch," I said, "without talking, for five whole minutes." So we approached the window; there, silently, we watched. The students on the other side appeared to be taking a test. A girl folded a stick of gum onto her tongue. Another kid scratched his temple with the eraser on his mechanical pencil. A teacher—a young woman— erased the whiteboard. I watched my students watching. "This is so creepy," one girl whispered, and when I asked her why, she said, "I don't know, it just is." What I wish I'd said, but didn't, was that maybe it felt uncomfortable to do something together that we normally did in private. It wasn't the watching of others without them knowing that we found "creepy," per se—we all watched others without them knowing all the time, and if we thought about it, we might arrive at the conclusion that we'd been doing this kind of watching for as long as we could remember. I could've asked my students if anyone had spent time recently with a baby, since a baby was the only type of human who was allowed to stare to her tiny hearts' content at other people without being shamed, at least until she reached an indiscriminate age, and her parents began—out of nowhere—to insist that staring at another human being was rude. I could have posited that the vast majority of my students had surely sat in a public place—a city park, perhaps, or a mall, assuming they spent time in malls anymore, which I doubted—and watched people go by, making up stories about said people based on assumptions about the things other people were wearing: jorts, weaves, mom jeans, nose rings, fox tails that had been clipped to the backs of their pants, whatever. I could have reminded them that they likely watched people all the time—on buses, in restaurants, in libraries, during football games—and that they likely stole glances, especially if the person being watched was incomprehensibly beautiful or, sometimes even more fascinating, hideously ugly—and that they did so naturally without even thinking about it, until they realized what they'd been doing and stopped, or continued to steal glances, albeit in a more covert manner. I could have attempted to lead a discussion about the differences between American homes and Dutch homes, and what it said about Americans that they were more likely to draw the curtains or blinds in the evenings, whereas the Dutch didn't even own curtains or blinds, and that their living rooms were stages upon which they proved they had nothing to hide. I could have provided autobiographical examples of my own watching, which would have likely included how, for ten years, we lived across from a house that was visited at least twice, if not three times, by a tiny little man who drove a tiny white pickup truck and carried two tiny dogs beneath each arm, and though we knew that the tiny man's brother lived in the house, we couldn't ever understand why the tiny little man visited so often, and so we couldn't help, when we pulled our curtains aside just enough to see him walk briskly from his truck to the front door, but suspect the worst. I could have shared the idea that one of my friends gave me, years ago, an idea I know that he got from somebody else but can no longer remember who, that we humans are what the universe has grown in order to see itself: 8 billion self-reflexive periscopes. I could have introduced a quote by a person who was a far superior thinker than I could ever hope to be, who said, "Time is the psychological enemy of man. Our action is based on knowledge and therefore time, so man is always a slave to the past. . . When man becomes aware of the movement of his own consciousness, he will see the division between the thinker and the thought, the observer and the observed, the experiencer and the experience. He will discover that this division is an illusion. Then only is there pure observation which is insight without any shadow of the past or of time. This timeless insight brings about a deep radical mutation in the mind." As it turns out, I didn't do any of these things. I was too curious about what my students had seen when they looked into the classroom next door, and whether or not someone had noticed something I hadn't, or if any of them had noticed the things I had also noticed, so I told them to open their notebooks and write down what they had seen during their five minutes of unabated observation, and after letting them scribble for a few minutes—surely not long enough for anybody to finish—I asked for a volunteer to read what they'd written. Then, I waited for someone—anybody—to raise up a hand.

# PRECIOUS METALS

Despite lying in a dark field for over an hour, I saw only four shooting stars during the Perseid meteor shower; I wanted to blame it on light pollution, but other humans live-tweeting it in less remote places said it was like watching "gods write with cosmic chalk" or "burning jewels melt." According to the Weather Channel, July 2016 was the warmest month on record, and the fifteenth consecutive warmest month since humans began keeping track. Sadly, I still don't know how—and apparently lack sufficient evidence—to convince people I love that climate change is not a hoax, and they're not the only ones who've been duped: LeBron James thinks that Michael Jordan gets too much credit for the Bulls' six titles, and a Knoxville man believed—for five years—that he was dating Katy Perry. Thanks to a Tumblr called "mcmansionshell," I now have a vocabulary for why so-called McMansions are such monstrosities: most of the problems appear to stem from the absurd imbalance of principal and secondary masses. In the last two weeks, I've spotted at least three dead birds on the side of the road: chickadee, a northern flicker, and a cardinal. At the Pete Dye Golf Course, where English department faculty had gathered for our annual retreat, we looked up from our brainstorming session on "experiential learning" and "diversity and inclusion" to watch a thunderstorm blow a blizzard of leaves past the two-story windows of the room we'd rented. According to a colleague of mine, George Gershwin couldn't stop smelling burnt rubber, couldn't get the smell out of his nose; what he didn't know: the scent was the result of a phenomenon called "phantosmia," an olfactory hallucination created by a brain tumor that would prove malignant. The other night, I dreamed that, in order to survive, I had to kill someone: that I had to eviscerate a fat man with a sword. Afterwards, I realized I was back at my old boarding school, and that my old girlfriend was living across the hall from me; I embraced her and woke up hugging a pillow. Later, I sent to a good friend who's unhooked himself from social media a screenshotted announcement about an upcoming novel by a writer we both know and whose ironic vanity, we like to think, is still vanity, and unwarrantedly so; this same friend, who once took a dump in a litter box and called his wife to come take a look at what the cat had done, was surprised to learn that Copenhagen was home to the most beautiful people he had ever seen—young blond models, radiant, sipping coffee in cafés—the sheer volume of whom made him feel, in his own words, like "a troll." As much as I envied his travels, I was perfectly satisfied staying here and walking the dog to the horse hill to view, at sunset, the green backbone of Brush Mountain tufted with clouds; this same view reminds a guy in my neighborhood of the verdant ridges in the Sri Lankan jungle he once called home, and where, on his sixth birthday, he woke to an elephant's trunk nuzzling his face—an experience that his father had planned as a gift. The man who helped engineer the sale of my family's old house and the purchase of our new one stopped by the other day to drink a beer and tell me that when he'd woken that morning he could feel the imbalance, that everything in the world—religion, government, politics—was off-kilter, and what he wanted me to know, what he felt he had an absolute responsibility to tell me, was that I should transfer at least ten percent of my assets to precious metals. I overheard a girl in the library stack say, "I can't even come up with the point of living anymore." The boy she was with said, "If you ever kill yourself, I would so die." "Me, too," she said, and when they laughed, I thought about someone I love who recently confessed that he'd spent twenty years of his life thinking about killing himself, and that if there had been a magic button he could've pressed that would've allowed him to erase his entire existence, without causing pain to anyone else that he knew, he would've pressed it. Several times, as I neared the end of a bike ride, I thought I heard a car approaching me, and gripped my handlebars tightly, imagining, as I almost always do, a car's bumper clipping my rear tire, or a truck's heavy-duty side-view mirror whacking me in the back of the head, but when I glanced over my shoulder and saw that nobody was there, I realized that what I'd heard was the sound of my own spinning wheels.

# PERMANENT EXHIBIT

Descending into the valley always feels like entering a secret world—but only when I'm on my bike. Today, along
the shoulder of Catawba Road, I noticed green plant life
receding. Streams slowing. Brown stalks on tomato plants.
The bottom half of a creek bed was bone dry, its boulders
chalky with dust. Someone said recently that the insect
world already sounded like autumn, and though I couldn't
identify a single contributor of the endless buzz that en-
gulfed me, I had to agree. Ash trees, a friend told me, are
the first to turn; I wondered if that explained the yellow
leaves on the parking lot behind the old Christian Science
Reading Room. I climbed a gravel road, dodging the bigger rocks, the way the spaceship in the game Galaga has
to swerve to avoid the bombardments of insectlike aliens.
I scanned the woods for the owl I'd seen a few days before,
the one who, in the dappled light falling through the forest canopy, flapped itself up onto a maple branch, turned
its head to look at me, then flew deeper into the woods.
Today, though, I didn't see it. Twenty-one years ago, on a
cold January morning, I saw an owl—it was snow white,
and though I might have been high at the time, I'm as sure
about this fact as I am about my own name—near the
"Right Loop" trailhead at Tsali Recreation Area in southwestern North Carolina. The owl landed on a branch about
fifteen yards away; we looked at each other for so long, I
thought it was daring me to move. I caved; it flew away.

The Tsali Recreation Area was named after a Cherokee Indian named Tsali, who, after Andrew Jackson signed the Indian Removal Act of 1830, refused to leave the mountains where he hunted and tended a hillside garden and lived in a cabin with his family—at least until a group of armed U.S. soldiers rounded them up. According to one account, a soldier jabbed a bayonet into the back of Tsali's wife, which prompted Tsali to communicate, in Cherokee, to his fellow men, to overpower the soldiers; in the resultant scuffle a soldier's gun went off accidentally, two other soldiers were wounded, and one of these eventually died, and in order to save his friends and family, Tsali surrendered himself as a sacrifice. According to another account, one of Tsali's men slipped out a hatchet he'd hidden in his shirt and sunk it into the head of one of the federal troops; he and the other men were later captured—by a group of Oconaluftee Citizen Indians, who had been granted permission to stay—and tied to trees, where they were shot by a firing squad. You can visit Tsali's grave—which is fenced by an iron gate and marked by a boulder bearing a metal sign—in Robbinsville, North Carolina, and afterwards you can visit Joyce Kilmer Memorial Forest, where you can stand beneath 400-year-old yellow poplars, some of which are more than twenty feet in circumference. During your visit, you can also read the poem "Trees" by Joyce Kilmer, which begins with the line "I think I shall never see / A poem as lovely as a tree" and ends with "Poems are made by fools like me, / But only God can make a tree." Presumably, Kilmer would have been happy to know that a National Park—one that now is home to the largest stand of virgin forest east of the Mississippi—had been named for him, but probably sad to know that, seventy-five years after the park's opening, the forest's hemlocks were devastated by the woody adelgid, and because the decimated trunks posed a safety hazard to the 40,000 hikers who visit the park annually, and because it is unlawful to use a chainsaw for any reason within the park's boundaries, the U.S. Forest Service used dynamite to fell them. One of my father's patients claims that there are secret Indian burial mounds at Joyce Kilmer; as a kid, I could never figure out why Indian burial mounds didn't get ransacked, in general, and by me, in particular. I don't know how long you have to be dead before it's okay for archaeologists to dig you up, but I like to think about in-the-future humans plundering my grave, wouldn't mind donating my body to science, as long as my skull became a prop on someone's desk, like the skull that used to sit on the desk of my Uncle Rick-Rick, who used it as a macabre puppet and referred to it as Mr. Bones. Perhaps I could arrange for my skull to be turned into a kind of permanent exhibit; using animatronics, the skull would live in a cube—in a museum? a cemetery? the family graveyard?—where its jaw would move, and speakers would play words that I'd written, and perhaps it would even read what I'm writing right now, and tell the story of the dead snake I saw on Catawba Road, and that I had seen it alive, in the same place, two days before: enrobed in lustrous black scales, and presumably attracted to the heat-conducting properties of the asphalt upon which it laid, in a luxuriant tangle. It seemed stupid to feel sorry for a dead snake, but no stupider for the wasps in the attic of my garage that I'd sprayed with Raid. I'd opened a hinged door in the ceiling and blasted a stream of poison at the nest, an assemblage of hexagonal paper cells affixed to the outside of the attic's vent. Immediately, the foam I'd shot dripped like toxic spit back onto my head; in my haste to lay waste the wasps, I'd forgotten about gravity. Neither had I expected that, as soon as I sprayed the nest, I would feel anything but relief, or that, when I shut and secured the door, I would do so not only because I wanted to avoid getting stung, but also because I didn't have it in me to watch the writhing of insects as they died, or to imagine how, moments before, they had been so industrious, so inexplicably engrossed in their building, with no way of predicting, in the end, what was to come.

# TREASURE BOX

While a hygienist cleaned my son's teeth, I sat in the waiting room of a dental office, reading the first volume of *The
Collected Works of J. Krishnamurti*, which collects the lectures and Q&As of Jiddu Krishnamurti, a man who, in the
beginning of the 20th century, was groomed by a group of
Theosophists (who called themselves "The Order of the Star
in the East") to be the next "World Teacher," a messianic
role that Krishnamurti rejected at the age of thirty-four,
disbanding the Order and returning all monies and properties that had been donated to his cause. Claiming no allegiance to any particular nation, religion, creed, or philos-
ophy, Krishnamurti spent the rest of his life traveling the
world doing more or less what he had been prepared to do,
which was "teach"; he preferred giving lectures over writing,
since giving talks was a more immediate way of commu-
nicating with people. In 1933, Krishnamurti told an audience in Stresa, Italy—a town in northern Italy that sits at
the edge of Lake Maggiore—that the source of humanity's
conflict had everything to do with its desire for security,
whether material or spiritual, and that human conceptions
of God were false, because they were merely "speculative
imitations," and that religious institutions had been based
on such falsities, and that differences of beliefs and religions
had been the source of suffering and war since the dawn
of humanity, and that until humans freed themselves from
the illusion of time and stopped trying to find security in

anything apart from understanding their own minds, they would be enslaved by systems that kept them in line by offering them an endless stream of rewards and punishments. For whatever reason—I assume it had something to do with the word "punishment"—I remembered how, as a boy, I had on occasion earned a spanking—for tormenting my sister or cavalierly disrespecting a household rule—which meant that I would be sent by my mother to my room while she retrieved one of my father's belts from his closet. Once this instrument—in lieu, I suppose, of a "rod" or "switch"—had been retrieved, she would tell me to pull down my pants and underwear; I would lie face down on the bed and my mother would use the belt to smack my backside. It's hard for me to imagine spanking my own son in this manner. I only spanked him on a few occasions and never with a belt; the last time I tried, when he was a toddler, he fought back with such ferocious desperation that I had no other choice but to think: *what the hell am I doing?* Even so, I never resented my mother for spanking me—maybe because she proceeded each time with such calmness and rationality; I had disobeyed, I had earned this punishment, and she was merely its arbiter. Afterwards, as a kind of reconciliatory consolation, she embraced me, then knelt down with me beside my bed. As I was remembering this scene, and how I would repeat, after my mother, whatever prayer she improvised—a door at the other end of the waiting room opened. My son walked out; a hygienist followed. "Everything looks good," she said. I raised my eyebrows. "It does?" I said, remembering how, whenever he had occasion to snuggle with his mother, she often asked him whether he'd brushed his teeth, because if the smell of his breath was any indication, he had not. In the parking lot of the dental office, my son confessed that he too had been surprised by the hygienist's news. I asked if he knew how many cavities I had; he said, "zero," and I nodded, remembering how, on several separate occasions, I had fidgeted in a dental chair while my father had administered sealants. As far as I know, my father never spanked me, though once he yanked me forcefully by the arm and led me onto our back porch, where he talked to me sternly about something careless I had said. My son raised his arm to show me a rubber bracelet, imprinted with the word "groovy." It looked like it'd been tie-dyed. "I got this from the treasure box," he said proudly, and when I asked him if he wasn't a little too old for the treasure box, he shrugged and said, "She said I could take something, so I did." I thought about asking him if he could remember having been spanked, but then thought better of it; when he turned the radio to K92, and began to sing along to "Don't Let Me Down," I didn't try, as I often did, to change the station—I just let it play.

# BLOOD SOUP

A friend and fellow colleague of mine, an industrial design professor and self-proclaimed vegetarian, once found himself at a Dim Sum restaurant in Changsha City, in the Hunan province of China, where, as the guest of honor, he was asked to be the first to sample each dish that was brought to the table, and which included, much to his dismay, a bowl of pig's blood soup. The other day this same man, whose last name always calls to my mind the image of a shark fin, sent me a link to an article about an artist—a sculptor—who has been building, for over two decades, a series of monuments in a Nevadan desert: triangular slabs of concrete and monolithic so-called "complexes" that resemble Mayan pyramids, all of which, the artist hopes, will outlast humanity. I was Google imaging this place and thinking about a friend of mine who confessed that he hoped whatever books he might write would still be read fifty years after he died, when a colleague entered my office and said, "Check your email," so I did, thinking that maybe he'd sent me something interesting to consider, since, in the past, he'd sent invitations to lectures ("Captain America as Literature"), and articles about writers who can apply for residencies on Amtrak, and jazz renditions of "Be Thou My Vision," but when I checked my inbox I found an email not from my colleague but from one "Robert Birdman" that said, "I am here to inform that in the next couple of days I will break in to (sic) the campus and will kill as many people as I can until the police

arrives." I stared at the name "Robert Birdman," then Googled it; the only Robert Birdman I could find was Robert
"Birdman" Straud, a convicted murderer who, after taking
care of a nest of injured sparrows he discovered in a prison
yard, became an amateur ornithologist. After agreeing with
my colleague that this was a situation worth monitoring, I
received a text from my friend Terry, a guy who'd grown up
in Blacksburg and attended Virginia Tech—and who I will
always remember sitting next to during George W. Bush's
address to the university after the April 16th shootings, a
speech we had watched on the JumboTron of Lane Stadium,
with the rest of the overflow crowd that hadn't arrived early
enough to claim a seat at Cassell Coliseum. Terry, a gamer
who regularly plays online with a group of Pakistani men
who own bodegas in New York City, and with a disabled
fifteen-year-old boy who lives with his grandmother in
Illinois, suggested that we "heist it up later" and "make
some clams," by which he meant "play *Grand Theft Auto V*
Online." I texted back, "Sure," then stared at my computer
and imagined a deranged "Robert Birdman"—I pictured
the bald head and avian nose of Robert Straud, whose picture I had just viewed on Wikipedia—on the Virginia Tech
Drill Field, mowing down people with a military grade machine gun. Several students emailed me to say that, because
of the Birdman email, and because they heard the campus was on lockdown—it wasn't—that they would not be
coming to class, and I wrote back to say that I understood.
I didn't know what to do myself, except to live my life as
usual, which meant teaching my classes, going home for dinner, and walking the dog while listening to Frank Ocean's
"There Will Be Tears," on repeat, a song I just discovered
and which is about how the singer only knew his grandfather—"the only dad I've ever known"—for a little while,

and at the man's funeral he had to hide his face, since none of the other boys—who were also fatherless—were crying. "You can't miss what you ain't had," one of them says, and Ocean responds with, "Well I can," then belts out: "I'm saaad!" As I watched the last splotches of sunset fade, I decided to call my own father, but the call failed, so I dialed again, and got sent directly to voicemail, tried again, same thing. Then I remembered: my father was with a group of local men on their annual trip to gather blackberries and eat steak and eggs while sitting around campfires at "the Bald," a grassy meadow at the top of the Snowbird Mountain range, in Graham County, North Carolina, a place that, in the early 19th century, George Gordon Moore, a self-made millionaire rumored to have been F. Scott Fitzgerald's model for Jay Gatsby, had attempted unsuccessfully to transform into a European-style game preserve and lodge that would cater to wealthy men who wanted the thrill of hunting and killing wild animals. Moore transported an ark's worth of animals to the Bald, including eight buffalo, fourteen elk, six Colorado mule deer, thirty-four bears, two hundred wild turkeys, ten thousand eggs of the English ring-necked pheasant, and, perhaps most significantly, fourteen young wild boar, shipped from Russia's Ural Mountains, a range that, it's worth pointing out, bears a striking resemblance to the Appalachian mountains of Tennessee and North Carolina, and may have something to do with the hog's subsequent proliferation, as the dark thickets of laurel and rhododendron provide the animal plenty of places to hide, as well as an abundance of food sources, including roots, acorns, and—according to a November 1961 issue of *Popular Science*—rattlesnakes, a delicacy the animal stomps to death with its hooves and devours "on the spot." Though the wild boar population has grown substantially since the early 1900s—they are said to be both destructive and, unless you have the proper weaponry, indestructible—and though I have seen evidence in dark mountain coves of their wallowing, I myself have never seen a boar, at least not in the wild. My father has seen them from time to time; once he approached an adult hog that had wandered onto his property and, using a .22 rifle, shot the hog point blank in the forehead. The bullet wound oozed blood, the boar wobbled a bit, but then turned around, and ambled into the woods, and though hunters were called to dispense of it, I like to imagine that the animal was not seen again.

# STORMBOX

According to CBS News, clowns have been making random appearances in Greenville, South Carolina, emerging—in one case—from a wooded area behind an apartment complex to whisper and make "strange noises," flash "green laser lights," and attempt to lure children, using "large sums of money," into the woods. Though I did not recognize the name of the apartment complex—Fleetwood Manor—I did recognize the name of the city, which, as it turns out, is where my mother and her siblings were raised, and where all of them, except for my mother, now live, including my favorite aunt, who become my favorite because she did things like let me eat chocolate mousse for breakfast and throw her long blond hair over her head like Cousin It from the Addams family and send me cassette tapes upon which she told me that she was sad to hear that I had not played with Teresa, a three-foot doll who lived in a back room closet of my grandparents' house, and that my aunt knew that I had not played with the doll because Teresa had told her so, and that the doll was so lonely that sometimes, at night, when everyone else was asleep, she slipped outside, to talk to Phillip, a statue in the shape of a naked boy who was perpetually holding onto a tiny pecker from whose tip a bit of black hose extended—ostensibly for use as a fountain, though I'd never seen him employed in this manner. Because I knew that my favorite aunt would have heard about the clowns— it was, after all, international news—and because I hoped

she might have some kind of inside scoop, I sent her a text
that said, "What's up with all the clowns?" A few seconds
later, she replied, said she didn't know, and that the whole
thing might be made up. What wasn't made up, however,
was the hurricane my aunt was currently watching on a
radar map at her best friend's house on the Isle of Palms;
it was headed straight for them. In an attempt—more or
less—to be funny, I asked if her friend had a "hurricane
closet," a reference to the "storm closet" that my aunt and
cousins would retreat to when my cousins were kids, whenever they received word of impending storms. No, my aunt
said, her friend did not have a hurricane closet, and in fact
I must have been mistaken, because when her children
were younger there was no particular closet designated as
such, though she did have something she referred to as a
"storm box," which contained a lantern and batteries and
a weather radio; during storms my aunt would bring this
storm box, along with blankets and pillows and candy and
games, into a closet, where she and my cousins would wait
for the thunder and the rain to pass them by. As someone
who has enjoyed, from time to time, hiding in dark places,
I always thought it would be fun to enter a closet during a
storm and listen to the weather radio and play cards and eat
M&M's from one of those huge, "family-sized" bags and
see the faces of my cousins lit by lantern light while thunder boomed overhead, but, as it turned out, I never visited
my aunt's house during a thunderstorm or a tornado or,
for that matter, severe weather of any kind. Still, I like the
idea of having a "storm box"—and although the kind my
aunt assembles makes a certain degree of sense, I think I'd
prefer to own one that, once opened, could actually create
a storm: I imagine lifting the lid, retreating to a safe distance, pressing a button on a remote, and wiry tentacles of

lightning shooting out crazily, into the atmosphere, where they would attach themselves to whatever clouds they could find, and tow them together, and then somehow produce the necessary instability and thus convection required to instigate a storm. Although I'm fairly certain no box like this currently exists, a Swiss company called Meteo Systems claims that their WeatherTec Emitter Systems can charge naturally occurring aerosol particles which are then "advected" into clouds by convective updraft, thus "influencing" ice particles and "enhancing" rainfall, a system that could be helpful—or so they claim—in arid conditions. Likewise, the Beijing Weather Modification Office, which employs over 37,000 people, claims to have the ability to produce rain by firing rockets loaded with chemicals into the sky, and "seeding clouds" to produce rain, as much as fifty-five tons of it per year. Of course, it is difficult to say for sure whether or not the rain that subsequently falls after a so-called "cloud seeding" is the result of nature or man, and as pleasant as it may be to imagine rain transforming scorched deserts into lush grasslands, there's no way to predict what the potential consequences might be, so perhaps it is better not to interfere, and better, in the case of an approaching storm, to seek shelter with the comfort of a storm box, or to do as my family did when I was younger, and as I do now with my own and only son, which is to find a place outside—a covered porch works best—to stand and observe the unfolding drama, far enough away from the main event to convince yourself that there's nothing to worry about, but close enough so that, as the rain mists your face, you feel the need for human contact, so you place an arm around your son's chest, which is itself a kind of storm box, if you allow yourself to think about your son's body and its capacity to act as a container of sorts and to imagine its internal workings as a kind of endless tumult, what with its ceaseless—at least until the day it ceases—flow of blood, the driving engine of which is of course the boy's heart, whose rhythmic and steady beat—especially at times like these, when rain-lashed trees sway in wind, and lightning flashes brighten the night—you are grateful to feel against the palm of your hand, as it is no more fathomable than storms, or clowns, or favorite aunts, or artificial rain, or dolls that come alive at night, or the fact that you emerged from nowhere to see it all, and to nowhere you will someday—but perhaps not just yet—return.

# GONG BANG CLEANSE

The last time I visited my parents, my father, who has been a dentist in a small mountain town for over forty years, told, as he often does, many stories. He told the one about a patient, who may or may not be a relative of blind country star Ronnie Milsap, who drank a case of Coke—two dozen cans—every single day. He told the one about a state trooper who'd been accused of offering the pretty girls he pulled over the chance to trade the tickets he was on the verge of writing for blowjobs. He told the one about the man who was struck by a semi while changing a tire on the side of the road while his wife and child watched, and how the man was then "chewed up" inside one of the truck's wheel wells. He told the one about the deputy a few towns over, a female jailer who'd witnessed female prisoners hiding things—a carton of cigarettes, an entire bedsheet—in various orifices, and who claimed to know a woman who loved drugs so much she'd have sex with just about anybody, sans protection, in exchange for said drugs, and due to her high fertility, had often become pregnant, and over the course of her life had pumped out twenty children, each of whom had been snatched up by the Department of Social Services, and that this so-called "drug baby" producing mother was just one of many. He told the one about the tiny widow who once asked him to fetch the gold from the mouth of her dead husband, who was lying in a casket at Townsend Rose funeral home, and so even though the gold itself wouldn't have added up to more than a few dollars, certainly not enough for my father to charge her anything, he'd gone during his lunch break to extract the teeth, but the funeral home was experiencing a power outage, so the staff members there opened the doors and rolled the body into the doorway so that there would be light enough for my father, who looked into the mouth of the dead man and saw that fluid had pooled in the back of his throat, to do his work. He told the one about a man named Purl, who was, at one time, the only black man living in our town, and whose legendary strength granted him the power and endurance to slaughter as many as twenty hogs in a day— killing them, dipping their bodies into boiling water, shaving the hides, gutting them, and butchering them—during which he filled and tossed back cups of blood, at least until he was shown, in Leviticus, that "for the life of every creature is its blood: its blood is its life," so Purl, from that day forward, gave up his beloved blood drinking. The story that meant the most to me, however, and the one that I kept replaying in my head, was the one about the old woman who'd been living for years in our old house—a house in a cove at the base of a mountain on a little hill above two streams, the one my parents sold so that they could build another, nicer house further away from civilization. At the time, the selling of this house had upset me, mostly because, over the years, the house had become essential to my understanding of the word "house"; in fact, to this day, whenever I read a story, and that story involves a house, and the narrator fails to give adequate details concerning this house's particulars, I automatically place the characters in the house where I grew up. At any rate, the woman—the woman who lived in this Ur-house—had recently died. Her demise, as it turned out, was swift, and had begun when she'd attempted to retrieve something from the utility room larder, the door of which, she was always happy to remind me, whenever I had occasion to visit, preserved the pencil marks that recorded the respective heights of myself and my sister over the course of a decade, and which had been drawn there by our father, who'd held a yardstick against the tops of our heads and made slashes with a pencil against the wood where the stick met the door. My father explained how the old woman had failed to grab hold of what she'd been reaching for, lost her balance, and fallen backwards, a fall that had been bad enough to land her in the hospital, where, perhaps because she was confused and desperate, she had tried to climb out of bed and fallen again, and broken more bones, and was subsequently transferred to a nursing home, where my parents visited her, and where she either didn't recognize them or pretended not to, perhaps because she was embarrassed to be seen in such an enfeebled condition. Soon afterwards, she expired. "It was like she willed herself to die," my father said. I didn't know that such a thing was possible, but I wanted now to visit our old house again, and when I asked my father if we could go, he said yes. I had no expectations of actually going inside, had simply wanted to walk its perimeter, stand on the front porch, and maybe follow the flagstone path to the springhouse, and scoop out a drink from water that my dad always claimed was "right off the lizard's back," but when we pulled into the driveway, a little round woman exited the front door, accompanied by a slender woman in her mid-twenties wearing a ragged felt skirt and tights, an ensemble that gave the impression that she might've just come from playing a role in a production of *Peter Pan*. The little round woman had known the old woman, and now she and her granddaughter were cleaning the house, readying it for sale, and no,

she didn't mind if we took a look around, so we did. Most
of the furniture was gone, and the floor was littered with
turd-like pellets. In my bedroom, I searched the ceiling's
plaster for the abstract patterns I stared at as a boy, before
I drifted off to sleep: the shapes of men with spears riding
horses with cartoonishly elongated legs, as if Salvador Dalí
had updated the drawing of the picadors from the children's
book *The Story of Ferdinand*, but as hard as I looked, these
figures were nowhere to be found. In the basement, which
the old woman had turned into a meditation room, I noted
the absence of our wood-burning stove, where my mother
had once cooked us pancakes after we'd lost power during
a blizzard. My father flicked on a light in a bathroom that
the woman had remodeled, and said that the old woman
had liked to fill up the tub and turn off the lights and float
in the dark and that it was, she'd claimed, like returning to
the womb, a desire with which, it may come as no surprise,
I could sympathize. When I thought about the house going
up for sale, and when I imagined potential sellers walking
through it, part of me wished that I could buy it myself;
what use I would have for such a house I can't say, though
perhaps, supposing I had the resources, I might have had
it demolished, which is the only thing I can think of that
would discourage me from attempting to make future visits.
Before we left, I noticed a gong—the size of a large serving
platter—hanging in the living room. I remembered that the
old woman had once claimed that the reverberations of this
gong had the power to restore positive energy, and since I
figured I might be the last person who would ever strike it,
I took hold of the accompanying mallet and swung.

# BRAIN BANK

My father is not in the habit of corresponding with me via email—he prefers, as he always has, to chat by telephone—but occasionally he will send, using his iPad, a hyperlink, and this will allow me to connect to something he finds notable: a recent mugshot of one of my former elementary school classmates; the obituary that included a photo of one of his patients who lived to be 111, and was pictured with a thick, torso-sized bible draped over her lap; a video taken by an aerial drone of the construction, fifteen minutes from my hometown, of the new Harrah's hotel and casino. Recently, my father sent me a YouTube video of a man who, in order to transform himself into a "dragon lady," had employed surgeons to cut off his ears, insert subdermal implants along the ridge of his brow, replace his nostrils and septum with slits on the sides of his nose, and then tattooed himself from head to foot with scales patterned after that of a western diamondback rattlesnake. I clicked reply and thanked my father for putting said "dragon lady" and its predictably vile comment stream into my "brain bank," the latter of which is a phrase my mother uses when she sees something on TV or in a movie—sex, violence, monsters, gore—that she doesn't approve of, as in, "I sure wouldn't want that in my brain bank!" and within seconds my father replied to say, "You've already made the deposit." To be clear, it wasn't that I harbored any ill will toward the dragon lady, since, as far as I was concerned, a person should have the right to do whatever he or she wants to his or her body, as long as it doesn't hurt anyone else; it was the comments that I found disturbing, and which attempted to paint the dragon lady and the doctors who'd agreed to help her with broad brushes; in some cases, commenters went so far as to suggest that the modifications she had made to her body were inspired by demoniac powers. In order to cleanse my mental palate, I scrolled through a news feed, and read about the giant holes that opened recently in the Siberian tundra. I read about the discovery of an Earthlike planet orbiting our nearest star, and though the planet is thought to be habitable, astronomers claim that the color of its sky would perpetually resemble our own during twilight in autumn. But I couldn't stop thinking about the dragon lady, or my father, who has always had a soft spot—if that's the word for it—for other humans who display unforgettable idiosyncrasies. Although it is safe to say that he could not be accurately described as "a lover of books," he did, when I was growing up, have something of a personal library, and among the few volumes he stored in a glass bookcase was one titled *Very Special People*, a book I never read, but whose interior portfolio of black and white photographs—a thirty-page section at the center of the book—I returned to repeatedly, as it included portraits of sideshow stars such as Grace McDaniels, the "mule-faced woman," whose face was severely disfigured, and Jo-Jo the Dog-Faced Boy, who was covered in hair from head to toe, and Bobby Kork, who appeared to have the features of a man on half of his body, and a woman on the other half, and a bearded girl, and a man who had a miniature twin growing from his chest, which was depicted both naked and dressed in a suit. There was the duo Tripp and Bowen, two men with mustaches and hats and suits, on a bicycle built for two, only Tripp had no arms, and Bowen had no legs, and there was Frieda Pushnik, a pretty woman who, though she had been born without arms and legs, could type and sew. There were Siamese twins, bearded ladies, a "living skeleton," a man with "elastic" skin, and Prince Randian, otherwise known as "The Caterpillar Man," "The Snake Man," and "The Human Torso," a man from Guyana who had also been born without arms or legs, and who, using his mouth, could roll a cigarette. I marveled at these humans, and though I pitied them, I admired them, too, for living, for having persevered. I had never seen anyone as stupendously different as these very special people, perhaps because medical science could now transform people and perhaps because the days of human beings featured at circus sideshows had come to an end. As a boy, I once visited a sideshow at a traveling circus that had stopped in our town, and planted itself on the same field where wannabe cowboys and their families camped during the annual Wagon Train, during which hundreds of people traveled from Andrews, North Carolina to Walhalla, South Carolina by horseback and covered wagon. I remember standing in line, holding a paper ticket, filled with anticipation, wondering what in the world an Elephant-Skinned Dog might look like, and then entering the tent and peering into a kind of cardboard cage, where a dog sat next to a basin of water. It was impossible for me to determine what kind of dog it was, but one thing was clear: it had been shaved of its fur, from head to foot, leaving it sadly naked-looking, and gray. I don't think this was the same circus where we watched a baby—a child who hadn't yet learned to walk—eat a McDonald's cheeseburger, after having consumed a bag of fries and a milkshake, but for some reason I can't think of one without thinking of the other: the first, a sad dog who couldn't make eye contact;

the second, a precocious eater of junk food. There is, of course, no way of knowing what happened to either dog or baby, and though their futures lacked promise, I can tell you nothing more than I have, except to say that that they live inside me, I carry them wherever I go.

# GAME DAY

Of all the animal carcasses I have seen on my bike rides this summer—snakes, skunk, raccoon, opossum, deer, newt, and a disemboweled frog whose uncrushed leg thrust itself out of a bloated mass of guts like a Swamp Thing append-age—there is none whose final moments of living I enjoy imagining less than the turtle. Something about the crack-ing of its shell and the crushing of its insides, subsequently reducing it to a flattened oval on the asphalt, makes my skin crawl. I've always liked turtles, always liked to watch them shrink into their shells, and thinking of them now brings to mind a cartoon—it may only have ever existed in my mind—from the 1940s that depicted the interior of one of these shells as a posh living room where a green, droopy-eyed fellow—the turtle himself—wearing a robe and slip-pers relaxed in an easy chair with a pipe and a newspaper, suggesting that the inside of the shell was much bigger than it appeared from the outside, an idea which, of course, would make a flattened turtle carcass all that much more disturb-ing, since who can say that this is not how a turtle feels, more or less, after he retreats into his home? Thanks to a dude at the local bike shop I frequent—a guy who is often wearing a T-shirt printed with the schemata for *Star Wars*' Millennium Falcon—I doubt I'll ever be able to hear the word "carcass" and not remember that it is the name given to the protective interior layer of a bicycle tire—one that safeguards the tire's sidewalls, which means that the phrase

"I am riding on two carcasses" now often enters my head, unbidden, when I'm cycling, as it did a few days ago, when, as I coasted down the mountain, into the valley, I had a bad feeling; on the other side of the two lane, cars were speeding past, sometimes five at a go, with little maroon pennants whipping on plastic sticks affixed to the driver's and passenger side windows. Inside, humans, mostly senior citizens, wearing clothes imprinted with university-approved logos, were on their way to the stadium. I couldn't help but think I'd made the wrong decision by traveling this route on game day; though there were no cars headed out of town, there were a great many headed into it. At some point, I would have to turn around and become subsumed by this traffic, which also meant that I would become something of a problem for the drivers of these vehicles, especially if they approached me as I was rounding a sharp curve, since, if they wanted to avoid the possibility of a head-on collision, they'd have to slow down significantly, at least until enough space opened up to safely pass. On any other day, I could've kept riding in my current direction; game time was approaching, and traffic would eventually die down. But thanks to the generosity of friends who had left town for the weekend and had to get rid of their tickets, I too was headed to the game, a gladiatorial contest about which I cared very little, aside from the fact that the event embodied the very definition of "spectacle": a kind of organized madness whose conventions were predictable but no less astonishing, thanks to the staggering enormity of the crowd, which, once the familiar riffs of a popular heavy metal song began to play, would soon be jumping up and down and howling inside a stadium that, what with its stonework and castlelike turrets, was truly colossal. So, eventually, I turned around. Knowing that cars would keep coming, I conscientiously kept to the right side of the road, clinging more or less to the white line that separated travelable road from its shoulder. A honk—sustained enough to sound indignant—made me flinch, and a red car, an American sedan of indeterminate make, passed me; the driver flipped me the bird. Because nothing sends me into an incandescent rage quicker than a bully behind the wheel of a moving vehicle, I flipped him the bird, too, cursed loudly, and began pedaling furiously. I knew it wasn't likely, but on the very slight chance that he might have to slow down, or stop, I thought I might catch up. I searched every driveway I passed, even though I knew that the people who lived on this road were less likely than those who used it as a thoroughfare to honk and flip people off; cyclists who glide from plateau to the valley are simply part of the world in which they live, and there would be no more sense in flipping off a cyclist than a deer feeding at the road's edge. I didn't know what I would say to the guy if I caught up to him, except to ask him, in as self-righteous a timbre as I could muster, what in the holy hell he thought he was doing, and why I, as a cyclist exercising his freedom to make use of one of my local thoroughfares, deserved to be honked at, much less given the bird. Already, my mind was generating assumptions about the bird-flipper: he was a meathead; a country boy; a self-congratulatory right-winger; he had a conceal carry permit; thought climate change was a hoax; used to play a little football himself back in high school; dipped tobacco and trashed the spit bottles before his girlfriend could find them; thought it wasn't possible, if a driver knew what he was doing, to drive recklessly, no matter how fast he was going; didn't like having to share the road with anybody, much less cyclists, especially if they fancied themselves serious enough to wear those corny-ass getups that made them look like flaming homos; and didn't much care for homos, flaming or otherwise, in fact would not disagree with the notion that gays could eat shit and die, or that they played a significant part—as did trans people, immigrants, socialists, hippies, druggies, and Arabs—in of this nation's moral and spiritual decay. I couldn't imagine how gratifying it would feel to tell him off, to get in his face and, surging with adrenaline, yell. Of course, if tensions escalated, I'd be a goner—I am not a fighter, and despite constantly getting into tussles and impromptu wrestling matches at the boarding school I attended long ago, I'd never had enough confidence, much less practice, to become a proficient fighter. I wondered then if maybe the driver of the red car was somehow in charge of this situation, that maybe it hadn't simply been a random bird flip to somebody who presented a less masculine version of himself, and that maybe the guy was waiting for me, like those fabled drivers who skulk around at dusk without headlights and who were actually initiates into "Blood" gangs, waiting for cars to flash their lights at them, an action that the driver of the non-headlight-burning car would respond to by following the headlight flasher, with the intent to claim the initiate's first murder. Maybe the antagonizing of cyclists was something that the driver of the red car got off on, and if one of the riders he flipped off shot him a retaliatory bird, the driver would park his car up ahead, and find a place to lie in wait, hiding behind a tree or a bush, listening for the zip of approaching bike tires, at which point he would step into the road and swing a crow bar or tire iron at the rider's head. I imagined glasses shattering, the astonishing burst of pain radiating from the point of impact outward, the skid of flesh against asphalt. I imagined playing dead long enough to hear the squeal of his tires as he pulled away. In such a condition, I wondered if I would be capable of tapping out 911 on the screen of my phone and, despite the blood burbling in my mouth, mumble, "Help." I would be too scared to touch my face, to learn the extent of the damage, knowing that despite whatever reconstructive magic surgeons might work, I would never be the same again. It may not surprise you to learn that this scenario failed to play itself out, and that the driver of the red car did not see me, nor I him, and no doubt I, as an idiot who would have the nerve to ride a bicycle on a road made for cars, am long forgotten, while the driver of the red car will continue to live a life inside my head, the inside of which, like his own, is far too vast to measure, filled with a stadium's worth of faces he has seen but never known, and ones that, despite his efforts, he will someday forget.

# EYE OF THE STORM

Maybe it was because I had been rereading "Emergency" by Denis Johnson, particularly the part where a guy named Terrence Weber enters an ER with a knife stuck into his only good eye, out of which he can still, rather miraculously, see—his other eye having been made of plastic or glass—but I felt a pressure that seemed to originate, somewhat painfully, from the back of my left eyeball. *This is it*, I thought, *my sight is finally going.* For years, I'd been bragging that, despite the fact that my work required the most careful attention to detail, I had never suffered any strain on my eyes, nor did I wear contacts or glasses—I hadn't worn glasses since I was eleven and misdiagnosed by an optometrist with farsightedness—and often added to this fact that the last time I had a physical, and read the eye chart first with my right then my left, a nurse wrote down in a file that I had above-average vision. The thing is, nobody I bragged to was impressed; they just shrugged or shook their heads or rolled their eyes, and predicted that the end—at least for my sight—was near, and that forty-two, actually, was the age when your eyes—if they haven't already gone—go. I'm forty-two. This is my forty-third fall. I am, more or less, in the prime of my life. I have good health. I exercise regularly, to clear my head but also because when my phone tells me that I've burned 1052 calories, I interpret that as a license to eat whatever I want. I send a check to a bank every month so that my family and I can live in a modestly sized, well-built home with wood floors and crown molding and sturdy doors and windows that open and lock easily. In my fenced backyard, there's a patio at whose edges I've plunged the ends of tiki torches. There's a fireplace on the outside of my garage. I have two cars. My wife loves me, and I her; our son has a big heart, quick feet, and a drive to succeed in school and at play. My walk to work takes me through a field where, this summer, clover and Queen Anne's lace and cornflower bloomed, grasshoppers flicked from plant to plant, and butterflies flapped crazily. I get paid to talk to people about art, and I know, every time, where my next meal is coming from. Although I sometimes worry that a stranger will unleash a semiautomatic weapon and start mowing down everybody within range, I don't walk the streets wondering whether or not I will be judged by the color of my skin, nor do I have any fear that a cop piloting a low-flying chopper will see me, with my hands up, and say, "That looks like a bad dude, might be on something." In short, so filled to the brim is my wealth that I can't help but imagine that there must be something lying in wait, just beyond the reaches of what I can perceive; another way of putting it is that it feels, sometimes, as if I have stumbled into the eye of the storm, and this gives me the impression—and of course it must be true—that a negative force might arrive to upset the utter calm and bankable routine of my present days, when I wake up and scroll through my various social media streams, pour myself a cup of coffee, and while my wife makes my son breakfast and lunch, then readies herself for work after saying goodbye to him, walk the dog around the neighborhood, up the golf course hill, where the sun rises above a field of wheatlike grass and pale blue mountains resemble frozen blue waves, and upon my return I eat my breakfast—an over-easy egg on toast spread with mashed-up avocado, with a prayer of gratitude that the drought hasn't yet impeded the rate at which I can purchase them—after which clean up the breakfast dishes, read—this morning I dipped in and out of a book of self-congratulatory poetry titled *Alien vs. Predator*—write, go to my office, attend a meeting, teach my classes, ride my bike home, pour a cocktail, play a popular song I've figured out, thanks to YouTube tutorials, on the piano, connect my phone to a Bluetooth speaker so I have a soundtrack for making dinner, eat dinner on a back patio while tossing scraps to dog, watch kid try to place shots on a backyard goal into the upper 90, help wife bring in dishes for cleaning, take the dog for a walk so as to check to see if tonight's sunset is worth Instagramming, hug my kid goodnight, watch television—last night we watched a Burmese python swallow an alligator, and thanked God we didn't live in Florida—until we can't keep our eyes open, then fall asleep, waking to start the whole thing—more or less—over again. I like to think of my body as being well, but I have no way to see inside it, and don't enjoy going to the doctor, and know that a body that seems more or less healthy can quickly fall into disrepair, as had the body that belonged to my father-in-law, who was one day carrying barbecue in Styrofoam clamshell boxes into his house when he fell in the carport and hit his head and his wife found him minutes later, dazed and bloodied, and how he went into the hospital, and how the doctors said that he had very little time left to live, because his liver was failing him, and how, when we'd visited him, he was out of it—you could tell by his glazed, vacant eyes—and how he would struggle to lift, with trembling hand, an invisible cigarette to his puckering lips and take a drag. What pleasure he derived from this phantom smoke, if any, I cannot say, but the image reminds me that no matter how much I promise to remember these days, they too will someday dissolve, the memory of them, like the memories of the indigenous people who once wandered upon the verdant plateau where I live, and like the white settlers who drove them away, and like the thousands of students who stream here every year to study and party, will be accessible only by God, and if I don't live long enough to devolve into a raving madness, a final darkness will envelop me, after which I have to admit I have no way of saying for sure what will happen.

# SOURCE MATERIAL

According to physicists, linear time is a construct created by the human brain. According to Elon Musk—a South African-born Canadian-American business magnate, investor, engineer, and inventor—our universe has one in a billion chance of *not* being a simulation. According to Space.com, the Rosetta space probe, launched by the European Space Agency in 2004, has come to its final resting point, upon comet 67P/Churyumov-Gerasimenko. According to INQUISITR, NASA's Mars Curiosity rover photographed a pyramid on Mars. According to snopes.com, this "pyramid" represents the effects of pareidolia, a phenomenon by which the brain sees patterns, including faces, that do not, in reality, exist. According to the Organist, the developer of Sirius radio created a robot built to resemble his wife, both inside and out—a robot that claims to "feel really real" and that thinking about getting shut down makes her sad. According to Maeve Millay, a character from HBO's *Westworld*, she does not, as a synthetic android, fear death, because she has done it "a million times" and is, in her own words, "fucking great at it." According to Philip Kosloski, writing for Aleteia, a worldwide Catholic network sharing faith resources, human beings do not become guardian angels when they die. According to Ellen G. White, the co-founder of Seventh-day Adventism, every person on earth has their own Recording Angel, who chronicles "with terrible exactness every wrong word, every selfish act, every unfulfilled duty, and every secret sin, with every artful dissembling." According to my mother, in a book whose cover was imprinted with the words "remembered joys are never past," and in which she used to record the observations she made as she raised me up in the ways I should go, as a child I loved to look at myself in the mirror. According to Lisa, a woman who called my landline to congratulate me about having won a trip to the Bahamas, it was true: I indeed had heard her correctly when she said, "the Bahamas." According to eyewitnesses and survivors who have reported welts reminiscent of sucker marks, the lusca is a half-man, half-octopus that uses its tentacles to drag its prey into undersea cave systems in the Caribbean. According to a student in my Contemporary Fiction class, getting only thirty likes in ten minutes after posting a selfie on Instagram is cause for disappointment. According to Microsoft Word, the word "selfie" is not a word. According to Harold Bloom, reading *Harry Potter* does not count as "reading," because there's "nothing there" to be read, only an endless string of clichés that does nobody "any good." According to a literary magazine I admire, the editors are grateful for having given them the opportunity of reading my manuscript and regret that it does not meet their needs at this time. According to my ring finger, I have a blood blister —a perfect ruby oval that reminds me of the jewels players collect when playing Voice of the Mummy, a talking board game that gives directions to players in a voice so deep and sonorous that it would come across as absurdly theatrical if its commands—which include "The black vampire bat thirsts for your blood!" and "This is where the spirits of the slain thirst for revenge!" and "The unholy snakes of Amon reach from below!"—didn't resonate with such darkly menacing tones. According to the undergraduate program coordinator of the department where I teach, if I don't submit midterm grades to the university on time, I'll be put on the "naughty list." According to my wife, crows should be called "little black sky chickens," and according to my thirteen-year-old son, people who ride in the backs of pickup trucks should be called "honkey donks." According to my friend Joe, Stanley the dog—a miraculous animal who, according to doctors, should've been dead four years ago, and who barked at me ferociously every time I came to the door, but subsequently took every chance to lick me that he could—died the other night, which I was sad to learn in part because I never got the chance to say goodbye. According to Henry, who is Joe's son, Stanley's heaven is a place where no thrown tennis ball will ever be lost. According to my wife, I am an idiot for joking that it should've been our dog who died, and not Stanley, the former being, as a dogsitter friend recently put it, the most depressed dog in our town, and the latter embodying, as my friend Joe put it, the absolute cliché of what people think about when they think "man's best friend," by which he meant that it would have been harder to imagine a dog who, with the right upbringing, would fetch and obey and stand at command for as long as it took to get a scrap of bacon. According to petshealth.com, "Dog rain boots will help keep your dog's legs and paws from getting wet, although many dogs will refuse to wear them." According to the Weather Channel, there's a hurricane with my name on it, and though nobody can say with any precision where it's going, it appears to be headed this way.

# CULT HYMN

Asked son—who was loudly singing to a song on his phone while dutifully completing his homework, which he does, every day, without being asked, as soon as he comes home from school—to be quiet. Son kept singing, so I yelled his name, got his attention, said, "Could you please stop doing that?" Had been trying to concentrate, trying to read something, and boy's falsetto was like a happy demon flitting about in the otherwise peaceful sanctuary of my mind. Felt stupid afterwards, like what kind of father tells their son not to sing? A self-centered jerk, that's who. A heartless doofung—a word the boy made up, and uses in lieu of the traditional "doofus"—who attempts to quash the childlike and improvisatory and developmentally necessary impulses that one associates with singing? Son suggested, correctly, that I should relax. Exact wording, if I remember correctly, was "chill." Rolled eyes. Shook head. Remembered telling own mother to "chill," a word that own mother always made fun of me for using. But none of this mattered, really. Regardless whatever ironic historical precedence might exist, still wanted son to stop singing. Did I know, at the time, that there is no human culture, no matter how remote, that does not produce musical sounds with the voice? I did not. But as it turns out, everyone sings—or has sung, or would, if they were so moved and had a working larynx. Even my wife, who, in her own words, can't carry a tune in a bucket. The first time I heard her sing, I asked her, point blank, if she was tone-deaf. This wasn't, I'll admit, the nicest way of putting it. Too embarrassed to say she'd didn't know, because nobody had asked her the question before, she said yes. I hear her singing, off-key, sometimes, but I don't have any memories of hearing her sing to our son, who himself doesn't remember the songs I sung to him as a baby in his rocking chair, the same songs my grandmother sang to me, in a warbling vibrato I did my best to mimic as I crooned "Little Man, You've Had a Busy Day," a song that was first popularized by Paul Robeson, who used his deep baritone to promote black spirituals and to benefit the labor and social movements of his time. Though that was my favorite song to sing, my son preferred "Hush, Little Baby," whose lyrics I changed to "Hush, Little Baby / Don't say a word / Daddy's gonna buy you a mocking bird / And if that mocking bird don't sing / Daddy's gonna buy you a diamond ring / And if that diamond ring don't shine / Daddy's gonna buy you a bottle of wine / And if that wine don't make you drunk / Daddy's gonna buy you a big fat skunk / And if that big fat skunk don't stink / Daddy's gonna buy you an ice skating rink / And if that ice skating rink burns down / You'll still be the sweetest baby in town." According to Wikipedia, there are multiple versions of this song; there are simple revisions to the lyrics, but all remain true to the promise of rewards for being quiet. As far as I know, there are a number of not-normally sung verses but no different versions of "The Star Spangled Banner," a song I used to sing, diva-style, with extravagant runs to steamroller my son's anguish during his diaper changes, which he hated. In 1989, when I visited Abidjan, West Africa, with my family, my father taught his sister's African gray parrot to whistle the first few notes of our national anthem, which it sang over and over and drove everyone crazy. My mother never liked repetition in music; if we rode together in the car and we were listening to a mixtape I'd made I became attuned to a song's tendency to repeat and anticipated, tensely, my mother's negative response. My father, on the other hand, can't believe I can't read notes and sing, which means that if I were to sing a hymn in church I couldn't sing the harmony, unless somebody else was singing it. The world's oldest song is a cult hymn, the notes of which were discovered on a clay tablet in Syria, and praises the god Nikkal, the Akkadian goddess of orchards, and wife of the moon god Sin, who had a beard of lapis lazuli and rode on a winged bull. As a kid in elementary school, when it was my turn to select a record, I always chose the *William Tell Overture*, by Gioachino Rossini, partly because it reminded me of William Tell splitting the apple on his son's head with an arrow shot from a crossbow and partly because it reminded me of the Lone Ranger, and I loved the Lone Ranger, though I can't say why, maybe the bullets and the mask but maybe even the song. According to Richard Wagner, "The human voice is really the foundation of all music; and whatever the development of the musical art, however bold the composer's combinations, however brilliant the virtuoso's execution, in the end they must always return to the standard set by vocal music." And according to John Koopman, whose website "A Brief History of Singing" supplied me with the above quote, "There are no bones in the human larynx, so archaeological remains offer no direct physical evidence of the vocal apparatus of prehistoric man." Thousands of years ago, boys rubbed flint together over bunches of dried grass to make fire, and probably, as they did so, they hummed, or warbled unselfconsciously, enjoying the warm vibrations in their throats; whether their fathers told them to stop it's impossible to know, but I can imagine a better dad coming up behind a singing son, his face aflicker with firelight, and gently cupping a hand over his progeny's mouth, then raising a finger to his own mouth, and—because words haven't yet been invented—pointing to his ear, and then they both hear it: a wail, a cry, the song of some distant beast who, now that night has come, is looking to slake its hunger, so get that fire going, get those flames higher, and as for singing, maybe it's best if you don't make a sound.

# THE SUBORDINATE FRAGMENT

Because I lived in the middle of nowhere in a cove at the base of a mountain on a hill above two streams. Because all the people I knew and talked to were white. Because all the native people who had once lived in these mountains three centuries before would have outnumbered those of us living here now, before Andrew Jackson signed the Indian Removal Act, before they were rounded up and marched by bayonet point to Oklahoma. Because whenever I heard the word "Indian," the first thing that popped into my head were those chubby guys from Cherokee who stood on the side of the road in red and yellow Plains Indians headdresses, gripping spears and holding feathered shields. Because Tonto. Because plastic tommyhawks. Because once upon a time I liked to sing along to the song "What Made the Red Man Red" on my *Peter Pan* record. Because the only thing left of that first civilization in our valley were pottery shards and musket balls and arrowheads, pieces of which you could find if you knew where to dig. Because the only real Indians were the few descendants of those few who were allowed to stay or those who stayed hidden in the mountains. Because kids liked to claim that they had Indian blood. Because me Chinese me play joke, me put pee pee in your Coke. Because my dad's Japanese and my mom's Chinese and I'm both. Because how many Polacks does it take to screw in a light bulb. Because kids turned their lips out and stuck their tongues flat against their upper lips. Because the only nonwhite person in our church—which was where the majority of our family's socialization happened—was part Mexican. Because the only black people I knew were from TV and magazines and therefore mythical. The Huxtables. The Jeffersons. The family from *Good Times*. Whitney Houston. Vanessa Williams. Jordan and Dorsett and Magic and Rice. Gordon from *Sesame Street*. Fat Albert from *Fat Albert*. *Sanford and Son*. Carl Pickens, the wide receiver from the town where I went to school, who ended up playing for the Cincinnati Bengals. Because Uncle Remus. Because one of my favorite books, as a kid, was *The Story of Little Black Sambo*. Because I could ask an adult to read it to me and not blink an eye. Because I thought the story was about tigers who take Sambo's clothes and then chase each other around a tree and turn to butter that Sambo takes to his mother, Black Mumbo, who makes tiger stripe pancakes which are eaten by Black Sambo and Black Jumbo. Because the word "General Lee" and the Confederate flag made me think of an orange Dodge Charger. Because a cross-stitched picture of a black man eating watermelon hung on a wall in our home. Because my grandfather—a man who'd lost the tops of the last three of his fingers when he was three years old and refused to move his hand from the chopping block where his sister was cutting wood, and then grew up to be a dentist who served as his own mechanic and took trips out west to ride horseback through canyons he read about so often in the Zane Grey books he collected—used the N-word. Because when I watched the NBA in his presence he stood there jingling the coins in his pockets and said, "I don't know why anybody would wanna sit there and watch a bunch of N-words throw a ball around." Because watercolors of black women in head wraps holding white babies hang in the houses of white people I know. Because there's a cute little figurine of a black boy in overalls toting a sack of cotton on my grandmother's windowsill. Because when I first read Flannery O'Connor's "A Good Man Is Hard to Find" and reached the scene where the grandmother sees a poor black child in a doorway and says, "Oh look at the cute little pickaninny," it felt familiar to me, like something somebody I knew would say, and had said. Because I can still imagine plenty of people I know saying it. Because my other grandmother, when I said I was dating a Korean girl, said, "Now, Koreans—aren't they the ugliest of the Asians?" Because we make up stories about people who aren't us. Because the majority of my students are white girls. Because a kid in my class wrote an interesting reflection about not knowing what he was going to do with his life and that this pressure was somehow exacerbated by the fact that he was the only son of Asian immigrants, and that this sometimes felt as if they had sacrificed everything for him, and that he'd ultimately be a great disappointment, but when I asked if he thought that he might learn something were he to write about all that, he wrinkled his nose and said no, he didn't want to write about being Asian, because writing about being Asian was so cliché, so expected, he just wanted to write about being a guy, you know, a regular *guy*. It may not surprise you to learn that this student didn't much like it when I quoted whoever it was who said, "Art should comfort the disturbed and disturb the comfortable," because the student didn't want to comfort the disturbed, he wanted to comfort the comfortable, wanted to be someone like, say, Phil Collins, because before Phil Collins, the band Genesis was overly complicated and like super weird but then Phil Collins arrived and dumbed that shit down, made it simpler and better and easier to like, the kind of music that was like pouring warm milk into your head. Because I didn't know what to tell him after that, and because I happen to like Phil Collins, and because it's not my job to tell him what story to tell, I told him that he should write what he wanted to write, and that if he needed any help, to please, by all means, let me know, though now I can't help but worry that I may not be the best person for the job, which maybe is why, when he left, all I could think of to say was good luck and goodbye.

# WE ALL GO INTO THE DARK

When I met the professor who would change my life, he was younger than I am now and did not look like a professor. I saw him in the halls of the English Department at the university I was attending; I'd noted his polo shirt, slacks, and backpack, and assumed that he was a "nontraditional student," the sort of guy who, having given up a career in managing chain restaurants, had returned to college to finish a long-abandoned degree. The professor did not wear a blazer or tie. His head—overlarge, egg-shaped—was thick with ashen hair. His eyes bulged behind rimless glasses; his lips were as pale as the flesh of his face. In other words, the professor did not look like a man with whom anybody could become obsessed. But what did I know? I'd only been on earth for twenty-three years. I'd recently moved to a generic Southern city from the middle of nowhere to pursue a master's degree in English. In my spare time, I picked up shifts at a local Record Exchange, pricing used CDs by artists such as Limp Bizkit and Korn and TLC and Whitney Houston and Goo Goo Dolls and Destiny's Child and Sugar Ray and Smash Mouth. I worked with a morbidly obese girl who couldn't shut up about local bands and a ponytailed redhead who loved ska and a short blond woman who loved Scottish chamber pop and a gay kid who loved shoegaze. When I wasn't working, I was recording reverb-drenched songs onto four-track cassettes, and reading books assigned to me by my Brit Lit professor, who answered every question we asked by saying, "Well, that's what you gotta tell me." I worked on stories for my creative writing class, which was led by a semifamous writer—a woman whose stories and novels took place in the hollers of Appalachia, a region with which I was well acquainted, having grown up in a house in a cove at the base of a mountain on a little hill above two streams. This writing class was populated, for the most part, by a number of older women who were taking the course because it was the semifamous writer's last semester before she retired and these women were such unabashed fans of her work that they'd named their own children after characters from her novels. I, on the other hand, was just happy to be in a workshop at all. I had no affinity for this particular school—a land grant university that specialized not in liberal arts but engineering and agriculture—and had applied only because its tuition was cheap, because it offered a master's with a concentration in creative writing, and because it was where the aforementioned semifamous writer taught, and I hoped she might take some special liking to me, as all my other writing teachers had, thus sending me up a rung higher on the ladder to wherever it was I was headed. Six months before, I'd been working as a receptionist for a public defender in my hometown, typing up complaints and emergency custody orders on behalf of impoverished parents, and filing paperwork for the desperate and doomed, like the guy who drove his car through the plate-glass window of an insurance company because the woman who worked there wouldn't return his calls, or the nurse who killed her husband with a shotgun, packed his body in a trunk full of mothballs, and went on vacation. It was in this same law office, where the lawyer would return from court, slice a few slabs of cheddar from a hunk in the mini fridge, dip them in a jar of mayonnaise, and begin chastising me for whatever I'd done wrong that day, that I received a call from the chair of the English department at the aforementioned land grant university, letting me know that my application for admission had been accepted. On the one hand, the chair found the low numbers on my GRE verbals "distressing"; on the other, he knew that words often caused a great deal of anxiety for creative writers. The department's decision, then, had been based on my transcripts and recommendations, the latter of which, the chair had to admit, were stellar. He regretted that the department couldn't offer me a teaching assistantship, but that was fine by me, since I couldn't imagine anything more terrifying than teaching composition to a bunch of freshmen who were merely five years my junior. A few months later, I became an English grad student, and a few months after that, I signed up for the professor's twentieth-century poetry seminar, thanks to a number of students I knew who had raved about it. On the first day of class, the professor placed his hands—fingers splayed—on the table in front of him. His head swiveled slowly, unabashedly taking in the sight of us, his students. "I can think of nothing more exciting," the professor said, "than human beings sitting down together to talk about literature." His expression, utterly blank, seemed to underscore the earnest seriousness with which he ushered this sentence into existence, and though I can't say for sure, I suppose I fell for him right then. We then began class, as we would every time we met, by answering, one by one, a question of the professor's choosing. For example: "What is your most powerful childhood memory?" or "At what point in your life were you most embarrassed, and why?" or "What is the most unspeakable thing you have seen with your naked eyes?" Once everyone had answered, we opened our books to the page where the professor wanted us to begin and took turns reading aloud. We read Wallace Stevens. We read Plath and Lowell and Bishop. We read Jorie Graham and Marianne Moore. The professor entered each poem we studied as if it was a familiar room in which he had lived for ages. Subsequent poems, he showed us, were simply other rooms, connected one to another within the enormous house that was the canon of Western Literature. In this way, the professor, like an enthusiastic tour guide, led us from room to room, revealing secret passageways in an ancient literary mansion that was forever being renovated and expanded, even as we passed through it. The professor talked about the poets we read as though they were old friends and, in some cases, he had spent time—real actual time—with them. He talked about James Merrill and his partner David Jackson, how they placed their hands on a homemade Ouija board and summoned messages from long dead poets. He told us about how Frank O'Hara scribbled poems on cocktail napkins during his lunch breaks at the Museum of Modern Art. He described how Wallace Stevens composed poems while walking from his house to his office in Hartford, Connecticut, and how the poet rarely traveled, except for annual trips to his beloved Florida Keys, and how he cherished gifts he received from people all over the world, as well as how he could spend an entire afternoon with an orange: studying its peeling, turning it over, relishing its color and the texture as light played upon its surface, the fragrant spray of mist as his nails tore into the peel, the sweetness flooding his mouth as his teeth bit into its flesh, and how these intensely present moments, for Stevens, constituted heaven, which meant that there was no need of another. During our discussions of these poets, the professor flattered us with attention, and appeared at all times to be completely absorbed in everything we said, never disparaging anyone, no matter how dumb our responses. If any of us offered a confounding or implausible interpretation, he'd say, "Where do you see that?" And if we said something stupid, he'd ask us to, "Say more about that." And if we said something funny, he would unleash a kind of unself-conscious machine gun giggle. And if we said something smart, he'd say, "That's genius." The frustrating thing was, though the professor demanded excellence, he offered zero guidance about how, exactly, we should go about achieving it; when we asked him what he was looking for in the papers we were to write, he said simply, "Be brilliant." And, because he invited us to visit him during office hours—to talk about our paper ideas, or to share writing that we'd written outside of the classroom—I brought him a short story of mine to read. This particular story had been based on a family I'd observed two summers before, while visiting a friend in Nebraska, and centered on a woman who'd married a former placekicker but had secretly been seeing a poet named Todd, a sickly looking dude who worked as a teller at a racetrack. "This is good," the professor told me, "but four hundred other people in America could write this exact story. You need to write the story only you can write." I was surprised by the frankness of this assessment; every teacher I'd ever had—including the semifamous Appalachian, who simply called my stories "wild" and insisted, without reservation, that she loved them—had always praised my work. Furthermore, I was surprised to learn that the professor himself wrote fiction; I assumed all professors of literature churned out literary criticism, and little else, because they had no interest in or lacked the talent to produce fiction or poetry. "I write constantly," the professor said. "In fact, I'm never not writing." Had he published anything?

He shrugged. A few stories, in respectable, if little read, journals, the titles of which, using library databases, I immediately sought out and tracked down, scouring each one for clues that might unlock secrets about the professor, whose voice, now that I was spending a couple hours a week in his office, often replayed itself in my head. His peculiar brain-tape unspooled phrases like "literature is everything" and "it's really the only thing" and "every story needs to be revised at least seventy times" and "there's no reason at all to write short stories unless they're absolutely amazing and unforgettable" and "I worry that you don't realize James Salter is God" and "I worry that you think someone else is" and "there is no God" and "when you realize this your writing will miraculously get even better." On this latter subject, the professor and I agreed to disagree, but it didn't make me like him any less, because he was—at least in my mind—a genius when it came to interpreting texts and connecting them to other texts, and making sweeping gestures about writerly idiosyncrasies like "most poets don't use kitchens in this way" or "that's never what a flaming cloud means." If it hasn't already been made clear, I hung on every word the professor spoke and latched onto every detail of his biography, which, for reasons known only to him, he was far less interested in sharing. Still, I learned that his father had been a famous professor at Princeton, a man who oversaw a cultlike following, and who left his wife—the professor's mother—for a younger woman who had been his student. As a child, the professor had visited Israel and been left alone in a hotel room, where, to pass the time, he read the Bible out loud to himself, hypnotizing himself with the Psalms, letting the words rush through his body like a kind of fevered electricity. The professor had graduated from an Ivy League school, which meant that he knew famous literary critics, one of whom was a personal friend and mentor. In the 80s, in New York City, the professor often stayed up all night, drinking and snorting cocaine and having intense conversations with people who were brilliant about literature. Those days, however, were behind him; he'd been sober for years. But he encouraged me—and others—to live our lives as he had, because we were young and could get away with it. For all these reasons—and more—the professor became my favorite person; there was no one in the world I wanted to please more, no one I would rather talk to. But the professor had a wife and two children, and I wasn't the only student in his classes who felt the way I did, as evidenced by the line of people at his door, and the way he had to say, when visitors overstayed their welcomes, "I have to kick you out now." In order to ensure a regularly scheduled sit-down with the professor, I signed up for an independent study with him, a course in contemporary American Fiction. We read *All the Pretty Horses* by Cormac McCarthy and *Been Down So Long It Looks Like Up to Me* by Richard Fariña and *Jesus' Son* by Denis Johnson by fall break, when, to visit a friend who was majoring in theater at NYU, I flew to New York City. This friend lived with her dollhouse-sized plumbing and appliances in a spectacularly tiny one-bedroom apartment above a pizza parlor on Sixth Avenue, across the street from the famous basketball courts. The professor, who loved New York, gave me an assignment before I left: "Document everything." So I did. While the friend I had come to visit was in class, I walked for miles, just as I imagined Frank O'Hara had, and as the professor himself would have done. There I was, in Midtown, walking through valleys of the shadow of concrete cliffs! There I was in Chinatown, eyeballing squid nestled in slushy beds of ice! There I was in the Metropolitan Museum of Art, viewing paintings from the 15th century: angels hovering on wings of exotic bird feathers, the Hells aswarm with aquatic monsters! There I was with my friend, high on ecstasy I'd scored from a kid back at the state university who hated that everybody said he wrote like Faulkner, even though he did! There we were walking at 3 a.m. down Sixth Avenue, which was as bright and teeming as rush hour! When I returned to the university, the professor asked me to read what I'd written out loud—he insisted that work be read aloud, whenever possible—and I did. The professor laughed. He said, "That's so great." He said, "That's brilliant." He told me to forget the reading for next week and instead work what I'd written into a story. So—because I did everything the professor asked—I wrote a story about a kid who, wandering around the Met, spots a cute redhead and follows her throughout the city, a story which, to my fragile delight, the professor loved. "This is why I will never be a real writer and you will be," he said, pointing out how I'd used the adjective "ribbed" to describe a water bottle. "You're on fire," he said. "Write another story and bring it next week." Even though I was not in the habit of writing a story in as little time as a week, I wrote another one. And then I wrote another. And another. And another. And another. And another. And in eight weeks, I wrote eight stories. Thanks to the professor, and to the tall, blond woman I met in a Shakespeare class, where we laughed like middle-schoolers at archaic words like "bunghole," a woman who would later become my wife, I felt more alive—and more purposeful—than ever. I was becoming—or so I imagined—what I had wanted for so long to be: a *writer*. I had but one goal: to keep going. "You'll get in everywhere," said the professor, when I told him I was applying to MFA programs, and he gladly wrote me recommendations, handing them to me in sealed envelopes with his name scrawled along the flap's seam. Because I decided, in the end, not to apply to one of these programs, and therefore didn't need the recommendation that the professor had supplied, and because I was burning with curiosity to know what the professor might have said about me, I opened the envelope and read the letter, which was succinctly evaluative in exactly the way that the professor levied judgments: "He is the real thing," the professor wrote, "I recommend him in the highest possible terms." As high as this praise made me, and as absolutely convinced as I was that one of the five schools I'd applied to would accept me, none did. However, I did end up striking a kind of gold: despite my lack of experience, I received an offer to teach from a small liberal arts college in Massachusetts, the same one that I'd attended as an undergraduate, so I moved to Massachusetts, where I lived in the attic of a 200-year-old house, whose space I shared with twin sisters and their one-eyed grandmother. I taught, and wrote stories, and pined for the girlfriend who would become my wife. I also kept in touch with the professor and continued to send him stories. In fact, for years after I had graduated from the state university, I sent the professor everything I wrote, printing out stories and sealing them in envelopes stuffed with SASEs so he could quickly send them back, which he always did, after marking them up and scribbling smiley faces next to underlined passages he thought were funny and drawing stars next to the underlined or bracketed sentences he found powerful. In some sense, everything I wrote I wrote for the professor, for the regressive sake of summoning those smiley faces and stars. There was nothing like opening the mailbox to find an envelope bearing the postmark of the city where the professor resided, or to open my email account to find a message from him. Inside there was praise: "I'm thrilled you finished *Gravity's Rainbow*. You have just vindicated your entire generation." There were morbid existential reflections: "Instead of happy birthday people should sing 'Dark Dark Dark They All Go into the Dark.'" There might be instructions: "I sort of want to see *Fight Club* but I never will. It's supposed to be funny. Tell me the jokes." There were disparaging updates about a class he was teaching: "Today people said that Stein wrote that way because she was rich. As if the minute they themselves got some money they'd turn into geniuses. Something they'd been putting off because they couldn't afford it." And the professor chided me for wasting time: "I don't really understand the whole concept of telling someone a story before you've written it. It's like saying, 'I'm going to write a song, it's going to go like this.' Just write it." He gave me encouragement: "You were meant to be a writer. You are prodigiously talented as a writer. OF COURSE you are going to sound like other writers. Occasionally it will be a little bit too much and then you have to fix that, which won't always be easy. You have to be psychotically thick-skinned until you make it and after." He scolded me for my impatience—"your stories, like mine and everybody's, need time and dozens and dozens of rewrites"—and offered summations of my work: "I never think of your stories as relentlessly dark. You yourself are as a person very happy and your very smart decision is to turn that happiness into linguistic energy. All your stories are essentially comic, I think. Many of them have moments of sadness but I think at this point in your life you know pretty little about loss." In short, it didn't matter what the professor said, really, as long as his direction was directed, however briefly, toward me. And after my wife and I were married, at an Anglican church

where the professor presided over the scripture reading, and
we moved to Indiana, where my wife would begin pursuing
a PhD, I began teaching first-year composition and reading
for the university's literary magazine, the editor of which
encouraged me to solicit work from writers I admired, and
because the professor fell into this category, I asked him to
send me something. Much to my surprise, he did. The story
was about a man whose wife had left him for another man,
with whom she had had a baby, and after the baby's father
had died, the woman moved in with another woman, despite the fact that the man—the first one, the main character—begged her to return to him. The story established
fairly quickly that this first man—who was the main character—had become unhinged: he saw snow falling everywhere and was visited by the ghost of his dead father, who
instructed him to visit the home of his ex-wife and to leave
said home with the ex-wife's baby. It wasn't just a good story,
it was the definition, in my eyes, of an absolute bona fide
masterpiece, and like all stories written by the professor, it
seemed to provide psychological insights into the enigma
that was his life. It didn't even matter to me, in the end,
that another, more prestigious literary journal accepted the
professor's story, meaning that the little magazine I was
reading for could not publish it. The fact that it existed,
and that I had read it, was enough. And though the professor and I remained in contact with one another, we corre-
sponded less frequently, largely because my wife and I were
now parents, with a new baby to take care of, a baby who
seemed never to be satisfied, a baby who cried and fussed
almost constantly, unless we were carrying him around outside. Once he had grown big enough to sit in a backpack,
I spent hours every day walking him around the Midwest-
ern town where we lived, in rain and sun and snow and

wind, because this was the only thing that would satisfy the boy. If I had to go to the grocery store or the bank or the library, I always took him in the backpack, and because he was a baby—an especially handsome baby—someone always smiled at us, or made a comment about his face or hair or eyes, or about me and what a good father I was, and the thought eventually occurred to me that these assumptions strangers made about me were absurd, because I might, in theory, be on my way to committing any number of crimes simply by taking advantage of the fact that I was carrying a baby in a backpack. Of course, I didn't actually commit a crime with my son in a backpack, but I did write a story in which a character carrying a backpack with a baby plans to commit a crime, and when I sent a draft of this particular story to the professor—I was still sending him stories on occasion, and he was still reading them and marking them up with stars and smiley faces and sending them back—his response included an allegation: that by using a similar piece of baby equipment as he had for a central prop in my story, I was ripping him off. In other words, the story that he had written about the man who attempted to steal his ex-wife's baby had shown up on her doorstep wearing a Snugli, which is a kind of baby-carrying equipment, albeit the type used to carry younger babies—namely, infants— tightly against the chest of the wearer, while I too, by giving my character a backpack in which a child is carried, had done something suspiciously similar. Not only that, the professor claimed that this was part of an ongoing pattern, that I tended to put stuff from his stories into my stories, and that instead of stealing from him I should do what *he* did, which was to a) steal from the great writers and b) people I didn't know. I reread the email. I stared at his emphatic instruction: "Don't rip me off!" It seemed like a joke. As if it couldn't be real. I had stolen it from life—my life!—and my life had been stolen by my mentor. I had written a story based on my experience of carrying a baby—my own child—in a backpack. I hadn't imagined, and refuse to imagine now, that I had borrowed—much less *stolen*—anything whatsoever from the professor; after all, the man in his story never carried a baby anywhere, and therefore the empty Snugli he wore to the house of his ex became a symbol of his powerlessness, whereas the man in my story was an actual father carrying an actual child, partly because the child was his own, and partly because he knew that no one would suspect a child-carrying father of committing a crime. When I replied to the professor with these concerns, he said that he had taken a poll of his writer friends (not mentioning my name) and asked them what they thought about someone writing a story using that same piece of baby equipment in a central way. They—that is, the professor's writer friends, whoever they were—thought it was a little bizarre, and wondered if I was just very naive or oblivious to the way writers treat each other. The professor pointed out to his friends that I had the same experience, and one of them said, "We ALL have the same experience. Everybody has the same experience." The professor then said that even though one of the most appealing things about me was my innocence, for god's sake, did he really have to explain how the fact that I'd written a story using that particular prop in a central way was bizarre? The professor then claimed that he constantly had experiences after which he said, "Wow, that was in that story by so and so. Now I can't use it." It would never occur to him to say: "Hey, it happened to me. It came directly from my own experience." The relationship between life and art was more complicated and subtle than that. Part of my experience, the professor said, was my experience of the story he'd written. How could I not know that? "Sorry if this basic lesson is a mindfuck to you," the professor concluded. These sentences bore into me as painfully and effortlessly as nails heated over a fire. *Don't rip me off. . . . Sorry if this basic lesson is a mindfuck.* The professor wasn't just my teacher; he had been, or so I'd liked to imagine, my literary father, a man whose brain, at least when it came to reading and interpreting stories and novels and poems, I admired more than any other. For years, he had engaged honestly and intelligently with my work, for no other reason, or so I had to assume, than to help me improve. I knew I wasn't his favorite student—there was a woman he praised openly and often in my presence who had published work in the *New Yorker* and who, much to my chagrin, had appeared in the "New Writer's" issue of the *Paris Review,* where the second story I'd ever published had also appeared—but I liked to think that I was at least *one* of his favorites, or had been, anyway, until now. I called my wife over to the computer. I asked her what she thought. She didn't like it, either. That is, she thought the charge was weird, that the professor was weird, that I should write what I want, that I should forget about him, that my relationship with him wasn't all that healthy to begin with, and that he probably was, deep down, jealous. But it wasn't that easy. I owed much to the professor. I knew that others had claimed he was manipulative, that he was jealous of other students, that he was capable of hurting those who admired him, but I wanted to think I was different, that I was a category unto myself, a kind of literary son, upon whom admiration and perhaps even love might be doled out unconditionally, from a reserve that could never be depleted. Even so, the next time I finished a draft of a story, I decided, perhaps because I wanted to avoid being stung, not to send it to the professor. Nor did I send the professor the next story I wrote, or the next. In fact, I never sent him another story, never again asked him to provide me with so-called feedback on anything. I did not email him regularly, and he did not email me. And so, in this way, we drifted apart. If the professor ever thought about me, ever wondered what I was up to, he refrained from asking, though if, on occasion, curiosity got the best of me, and I sent out a short email, as a kind of exploratory probe, he would supply, after a time, an obligatory message: what he was teaching, what he'd been reading, the last best film he'd seen, etc. But even these bare-bones missives resonated with the stentorian authority of a voice steeped in the drama of the literary life, which was, for me, the central essence of his power and allure. Years passed. My wife and I and our son moved to a plateau in the Blue Ridge Mountains, to work at the university where we still teach. Eventually, I published a book. Even though I hadn't spoken to the professor in years, I decided to send him a copy. After all, no one else had a more significant influence on my writing; without him, I supposed, the book would never have been written. I didn't expect him to respond, much less to take the time to read it, but a few months later I opened my computer and found an email bearing the professor's name. The message inside was brief, just long enough to say that he had indeed read my book and found it to be "fantastically conceived, if not perfectly executed." In fact, he said, he wished he had written it. I stared at this message, in much the same way I had stared, a decade before, at the phrase "Don't rip me off!" I wanted to believe that what the professor said was true, and that I had finally become what I'd dreamed long ago of becoming, i.e., the kind of writer who'd earned, through hard work and determination, the professor's unabashed admiration, and though I read the words "fantastic" and "not perfectly executed" over and over, I couldn't quite believe either was true, the good or the bad. I worried—as I do to this day—that it was some kind of backhanded compliment, that he was both telling me exactly what I wanted to hear and taking it back, all the while knowing that the mixture of praise and criticism would have a stupefying effect upon me and cause me to leave him alone. After all, he once said, when I complained about some of my fellow students in one of my creative writing classes, that I shouldn't worry too much about their various insufficiencies, because most people who took creative writing classes were morons and what all of them longed for—secretly, shamefully—was abuse, verbal mostly, and oceans of it. At the time, his remark made me laugh, because I thought it might be true, and because the professor had almost always seemed right, even when he was wrong, but also because I no longer thought—not even for a minute—that he might be talking about me.

# BLACK MAGIC

Mrs. Bilbo, my first and best teacher, presided over grades one through five at Murphy Adventist School, a two-room A-frame that sat upon a hill, not far from a church whose members worshipped on the seventh day of the week, as God had commanded the Israelites, in Exodus 20, to do. Mrs. Bilbo had freckled arms and short, curly, strawberry blond hair. She kept a wadded Kleenex in the pocket of her calf-length skirt and left very little fruit on an apple core, eating down to the stem and seeds. The giant notecards upon which our memory verses appeared showcased her perfect handwriting, and whether she was standing at the chalkboard, using that four-pronged instrument to simultaneously draw musical staff lines, or sitting at her desk, grading our exams and phonics worksheets, she exhibited the very best posture; as a rule, Mrs. Bilbo did not slouch, nor did she permit others in her presence to do so. I can't remember anyone ever making fun of her name, and if any of us had read *The Hobbit* and made the connection between hers and the name of that book's protagonist, it was never mentioned. Thanks to Mrs. Bilbo, my classmates and I learned how to say the Pledge, fold the flag, write in cursive, memorize the 23rd Psalm, and identify the birds that arrived at our feeder, which stood outside the large window behind Mrs. Bilbo's u-shaped desk: nuthatches, titmice, cardinals, goldfinches, and wrens. We also learned how to play "black magic," a game we reserved for rainy days, or when Mrs. Bilbo deemed it too cold to go outside. I can't remember if we played black magic on the day of the tornado warning, when low black clouds turned the morning dark as night, and the windows reflected a ghostly version of our classroom, but we might've. And I can't remember how the game started, though I expect somebody got excited about having recess inside and said, "Can we play black magic?" a suggestion that enlivened the rest of us, because black magic represented the kind of activity children loved most: the attempt to unlock a mystery, and also to preserve it. Those who were smart enough to have solved the game's central enigma took turns as guessers, exiting the classroom while the rest of us took turns to select, in secret, an object that the guesser would attempt to identify: an eraser, Misty Dawn's moccasin, the zipper on the side pocket of Tommy's shoe, the red barrette in Dorena's hair, the zebra at the end of the illustrated alphabet that lived above our chalkboard. Once the secret thing had been selected, we summoned the guesser—for some reason, I always imagine this role being played by Chris Brunner, a mischievous kid who surreptitiously shot other kids the bird and bragged about smoking rabbit tobacco—back into the room. Since Mrs. Bilbo was in charge of the game, she served as our interrogator, and began pointing to random objects, so as to present them to the guesser for his consideration. Was it that paper snowflake taped to the window? The guesser might tilt his head, might even shut his eyes, as if using his mind to see into the object, and thus verify whether or not it was the one we had chosen, but of course it wasn't, since a.) the actual rules of the game dictated that the chosen object could never be the first thing Mrs. Bilbo pointed to, and b.) the unspoken rules dictated that our leader must take, if for no other reason than to increase suspense and thus dramatic tension, a circuitous route through a series of things we hadn't selected to reach the actual thing we'd chosen. Well, Mrs. Bilbo might say, sashaying across the room, is it this math book? Not likely. Could it be this empty milk carton? Hm, the guesser might say, tapping a finger on his pursed lips, No. Then is it Donnie's erasable pen? Nah. The chore wheel on the door to the utility closet? Nope. Was it this part of the wet vac—the black nozzle? Ha! No way. Was it Jolene's dental appliance, sitting on a napkin atop her desk? Yes, the guesser said, and in fact *it had been*. How did the guesser know? Those of us who hadn't unlocked the mystery begged someone—anyone—to reveal it to us, but nobody ever did, perhaps because knowing the secret of black magic granted to these knowers a kind of power, one that would be diminished were they to reveal it. It strikes me now as significant that we were allowed to play a game called "black magic," since, as a Christian school, we were taught to eschew anything that reverberated with the slightest suggestion of the supernatural; certain children, I knew, did not celebrate Halloween, and some, I think, did not celebrate Christmas, because the placing of a lighted tree in one's house had its origins in the pagan world. There were a great many other things we could not do, like say, "gosh" or "gee," because they were euphemisms for "God," and thus would constitute the taking of the Lord's name in vain, nor could we say, "oh my goodness," because we were sinners and couldn't be said to truly have any goodness in us; as the prophet Isaiah had determined, our righteousness was as "filthy rags." We could not listen to the *Your Story Hour* cassette titled "Footprints," because it told a story with mature themes, which of course was the reason that Chris Brunner always tried to choose it. But we could play black magic, perhaps because it wasn't magic at all. I don't remember how I figured out the secret to black magic, if I raised my hand frantically—as those had who thought they had figured it out, scrambling towards the front of the classroom to whisper their hypothesis into an ear of Mrs. Bilbo, whose eyes darted back and forth while she listened, but eventually I did solve the mystery, and the game became fun in a different way: instead of being in the thrall of the unknown, I was a knower, a smug master who, with Mrs. Bilbo's guidance, could dazzle the unenlightened with my superior brain. The sad thing, of course, was that once the mystery had been solved, there was no going back; I couldn't return to that state of unknowing, nor could I experience the drama of wondering whether the guesser would succeed in choosing the correct object—or marvel at the how. I suspect that those of you who know the secret of the game understand what I mean, and if you don't, perhaps you expect me to disclose it here. It would please me to say that, in order to remain true to the spirit of the game, I must remain silent, but the truth is, in describing the game, I have already revealed its secret, which, as always, is not hidden at all, but presents itself every time, in plain sight, for all who have eyes to see.

# TIGER MOTH

I wanted to write about the psychological effects of a recent drought but didn't want to begin with either the idea of rain or the lack of it; I wanted to start with the fact that the vast majority of woolly bear caterpillars I'd seen recently were orange. Not mostly orange, with two black ends, as I had learned as a child to recognize them, but completely and totally orange, from head to toe, that is, if a woolly bear caterpillar—the larva of the *Pyrrharctia isabella*, or Isabella Tiger Moth—could be said to have either heads or toes, which, perhaps, they cannot. I couldn't remember having seen a woolly bear caterpillar that was completely orange, and figured the one that had appeared before me, as I was racing along on my bicycle, was an anomaly, some variety of larval mutant, but then I spotted a second and third and fourth completely orange woolly bear, each one dutifully traversing the expanse of asphalt before them like a tiny sock that had come to life. Once I returned home, I typed "woolly worm" into an Internet search engine and learned how some observers of the species had surmised that worms who had a higher orange to black ratio indicated that the coming winter would be mild, and though scientists claimed that there was little to no evidence to support the idea that a woolly worm could function as a predictor of any weather or non-weather related event, neither was there evidence to the contrary. Still, the sight of these orange caterpillars, and the mild winter they might or might not portend, troubled

me. I should say that I have come, over the years, to relish
excessive amounts of snowfall, and thus the necessary conditions for cross country skiing, an outdoor activity enjoyed
by those who have enough disposable income to purchase
poles and boots and skis, as well as the gumption, as my
ninth-grade Algebra teacher might have put it, to transform
what might otherwise be thought of as an inhospitable en-
vironment into a veritable wonderland: imagine shushing
past evergreens laden with snow and generating enough
energy that you end up de-gloving and admiring how falling snow crash melts on your bare hands like ice on a hot
stove. I should point out here that thinking about snow after having considered the woolly bear caterpillar was especially delicious because it happened to be late September,
and almost no rain had fallen in three weeks, and this lack
of rain had me worried, because as much as I dislike the idea
of a mild winter, I dislike droughts even more. I don't like
metaphorical droughts—reports about once-hot basketball
players entering shooting slumps, or stories about writers
who seem to have exhausted their figurative wells—and I
don't like literal ones. For some reason, the first thing I think
of when anyone utters the word "drought" is Mountain Lake,
on Salt Pond mountain, which dried up in 2009, a fact I
know to be absolutely true, because I paid this so-called lake
a visit when it shrank to its lowest point, and traversed its
cracked bottom, which was strewn with antique beer cans
that boaters of yore had tossed from their rowboats, and I
observed firsthand the puddle of dead fish that represented
the last of the lake's pathetic content. I don't like how dead
grass crunches during a drought, or how soil turns to pow-
der, or how the forest, as my father says, becomes "tinder
dry," a phrase that always makes me imagine the hot coal
of a discarded cigarette turning crispy undergrowth into a

raging inferno. Every dry creek bed makes me remember Volume 3 of *My Bible Friends*, a book I read as a boy that told, using painted illustrations that were as real to me as photographs, the story of the prophet Elijah, and how, after he spoke against King Ahab, he retreated to the Brook Cherith, which dried up; I can still see that dry creek bed in my mind, and the gray sky above, and the leafless trees, and the gray rocks which, only a page before, had been flooded with water, just as I can see Elijah himself, portrayed as an older Caucasian man receiving food from the crows that were sent by the Lord to deliver food. I find myself thinking during droughts about trees and how many gallons of water each one requires, and how they become stressed and how, to survive, they shed their leaves, and how much more water than average must be required by the enormous oak in the yard across the street from where we live, a tree that was purchased, seventy-five years ago, as a sapling at Sears Roebuck and Co., or at least that's what Doris, my ninety-five-year-old neighbor, has told me. As it turns out, however, despite all my worry about the drought, it did finally rain, quite a bit over the course of several days, so much in fact that the ground below our house became saturated with water, which began to seep through the concrete in our basement. Though I was distraught to learn that *The Red Book*—an expensive tome the size of my torso that my wife had purchased for me one Christmas, and which contained a facsimile of Carl Jung's visions and imaginings from the early 20th century—had been damaged by this seepage, I didn't mind using a wet vac to suck up the puddle in our storage room, since it meant that, in no uncertain terms, the drought was over; for days, we couldn't cross the lawn without leaving prints in the ground, which was so saturated it sucked at our shoes. But that was over a month ago now, and very little rain has fallen since, and so my mind turns again to the prophet Elijah, fed by crows at the edge of the Brook Cherith, during the time of no rain, hoping to survive. I think now about the tiger moth larvae, which, during periods of intense cold, produces a cryoprotectant, an antifreeze protein that protects its cells so that it can safely freeze. And although droughts and frozen tundra might be seen as vastly different, it seems they might have more than one thing in common, and perhaps the next time I find myself cocooned in worry, I will remember this little worm in the snow, with its frozen guts and heart of ice, waiting, without a thought in its head, for the next thaw to come.

# INFERNO

The mountains of my home state—the same state whose legislators believe protecting straight people from transgender people is more important than raising teachers' salaries—are on fire. The mountains where I live now certainly could be; we haven't had any rain to speak of in over a month. I keep picturing the U.S. Drought Monitor website in my head, wondering how long it will be until our part of the state will go from yellow to red. It's the 18th of November and pulsing swarms of gnats still appear in midafternoon. The maple trees downtown still look like they're on fire. Forest floors are so brittle that the depiction, in words, of the sound of anything that moves in the woods now would require an exclamation mark. I passed a grove of oak trees today on my bike and the leaves hissed. On a nearby ridge, somebody discharged a shotgun, then discharged it again. A truck from the Sheriff's office rolled behind two men in orange jumpsuits picking up refuse with trash grabber sticks. I wondered how long my consciousness would continue to unspool if I swerved in front of a school bus, whose chains clanked together ominously as it passed, as if it might be some kind of Dickensian ghost vehicle. I wondered about the signs I passed: a rusted square hanging from a pole in front of a barn that said "PET"; a flag advertising "fast Internet"; a banner protesting the proposed gas line that announced I had entered what might someday be known as "the evacuation zone." I thought about my students, many of whom would be spending Thanksgiving with family members responsible for electing the new president, for whom they could not bring themselves to vote, for reasons they dared not share with their parents. I wanted to tell the woman who comes to clean our house that I didn't vote for the President-Elect and that I hope she's not afraid, but my Spanish is worse than her English, so I left the house before she was scheduled to arrive, and sent her a text message to let her know the front door was open. On *The Diane Rehm Show*, Diane asked John Grisham whether his extraordinary wealth qualified him as one of the 1% of the 1%; John Grisham said he didn't know what that meant, and furthermore, could we just not talk about money or politics? Because, John Grisham said, he was *so* sick of talking about politics. My neighbor texted me to let me know that the pig he's buying will soon be ready for slaughter, and that my wife and I had been invited to their house for dinner and to watch *Survivor*, a show we don't normally watch, but we agreed, under the circumstances, to give it a shot. At the end of my bike ride, I glided into the cemetery I always pass on my way home, but had never actually visited, and was surprised to learn that none of the names—Savage, Mast, Shaver, Hunter—meant anything to me. I called my father to check up on the fires, which were now threatening to burn the historic Trail of Tears, which the Cherokee had walked nearly 180 years before, at the bayonet points of U.S. soldiers. The air, he said, was smoky. The forecast for rain was slim. The fires, according to some, could burn throughout the winter—and beyond.

# FAT KID

Sometimes I think about this kid I once knew, this boy who was fat. Like really fat. Obese, I guess, is the word. Not morbidly obese, I don't think, but I can't say for sure. I'm not a doctor. I can't observe the particulars of a body—human or otherwise—and tell you whether or not it may or may not be teetering on the verge of extinction. I do, however, have eyes. I like to think—and in fact I feel pretty confident in saying—that I know overweight when I see it. So, like I said . . . this kid, he was fat. In fact, I'd say that he belonged to a specific category: the kind that elicits pity. The kind you look at and say, what chance does a kid that fat have? It's terrible to think, I know, and worse to say. And it's not like I have a lot of room to talk. I could stand to lose a few. But still. This kid? *His* fatness? Whole other story. Wherever he went, the fact of that fatness was, if you'll pardon the expression, the elephant in the room. I'm not saying he was like those thousand pounders whose corpses have to be airlifted out of their bedrooms, just that this kid's fatness was something you would've had no chance of not noticing. You could tell yourself that you weren't going to judge, but I'd bet a dollar to a doughnut you couldn't help wondering how someone, specifically a child, could get *that* big. Was it the fault of his parents? His pediatrician? Was he somehow genetically predisposed? Was his problem—supposing you wanted to distinguish it as such—glandular in nature? What and how much did he snitch when nobody was looking? Did he get in trouble for raiding the pantry or refrigerator? Did he sneak out to the nearest convenience mart, where a raspy-voiced woman with bloated eyebags and a diamond ring on her finger rang him up and called him "Hun" when she asked for the total, and if so did this make the fat kid feel good, if only because it seemed to him then that in the cashier's eyes he was a regular person like anybody else, living in a world where all people were potential "Huns," and did he then give her a handful of quarters and say, "Keep the change," and ferry the snack cakes to his room where he stuffed each one whole into his mouth, not eating as fast as he possibly could, but with a steady consistency that still might have been accurately described as "wolfing," little beads of sweat breaking out on his forehead and air whistling through his nose as he chewed, not even really enjoying it except for the fact that he knew he shouldn't do it, but fuck it, who was he to deprive himself of this one joy in life, not that he didn't only have one joy, but this was one only he knew about, a secret joy, the way his teeth cracked the brittle icing and then squished into the yellow cake and the gooey filling and maybe he had a chocolate milk to wash down each massive bite, who knows? Maybe all he needed to do was get through the eating and emerge on the other side. But maybe I'm getting it all wrong. Maybe the only thing to say about any of this is that it's wrong to see a kid and think first and foremost the word "fat," wrong to imagine that said kid was somebody who lacked the necessary willpower to be *not fat*, the kind of person who couldn't control his desires. Aren't we all guilty of indulgence? Don't we all practice our own singularly ludicrous acts of self-sabotage? And might the only difference between our sins and his be that the consequences of his provide more physical evidence? What if, for instance, every time we got angry, our bodies started, ever so slightly, to balloon? What if we evolved somehow so that we grew what scientists would later dub, on the cover of *Time* magazine, "the fat gland," and that every time you lost your temper, every time the Dream Team lost to the Sacramento Kings in NBA2K14 or if your spouse washed something that shouldn't have been washed and dried or if your kid took too long finding a jacket to wear because he's pathologically slow in the mornings and the bus will be here any minute, what if every time you got mad this little gland secreted something, like fat, maybe, or cellulose, or whatever, and what if bodies started metabolizing—or not—anger or sadness or lust? In other words, what if you could get fat in ways other than eating too much and not exercising enough or having the wrong kind of metabolism? What I'm saying is, what if it had to do with something other than metabolism or genetic dispositions or food? Might you change your tune? Could you then eavesdrop upon our fat young friend as he confesses knowing how to make a "mean" spaghetti sauce without wondering what the everloving fuck he was doing making spaghetti sauce, regardless of said sauce's intensity or flavor profile, or what hole he'd been living in that would have prevented him from having heard that he, as a person of extraordinary girth, should be avoiding carbs and instead be subsisting mostly on a diet of nuts and fruits and vegetables and grains? Then again, do you have any room to talk about willpower? Do you know a thing or two about deprivation? Do you assume it would be no big deal to survive, say, on a diet of apples, just as a man I know named Junior once did, a guy who recently arrived to de-branch the trees in my yard, a guy who was certainly not, by any measuring stick, slim, but who, having learned that a person can eat as many apples as he or she wants and still lose an extraordinary amount of weight, embarked upon such a diet, and so for days and weeks ate nothing but apples, one after the other, just and only apples the entire livelong day, and that by doing so he shed—"burned it up," is how he tells it—an extraordinary amount of body fat, and is now lighter on his feet than he's been in years? Could you imagine a world where people like Junior took stock of their lives, and of what they might stand to lose, and then lost it? Is it too much to think we could teach ourselves to look at a person without inserting "fat" or "thin" or "black" or "white" or "straight" or "spiny" or "sticky" or "bedraggled" or "clean"? Might we learn to relinquish our hold on our qualifiers? Might someday we see a kid of a certain size and circumvent the adjective altogether, going straight—as we ought—to "person"? I'm tempted to say—sad as it sounds—that the premise sounds preposterous. But then I think of Junior, a once ground-bound body who regained, through sheer will, his mobility, and who now scampers nimbly up tree trunks with a chainsaw in tow, and once he gets high enough he begins what he climbed up to do, which is to say he chooses which limbs need to go, lops off the excess, making trees lighter, opening them up so that more sun can shine through to the yard down below, so that the grass there can grow once again richly green.

# HERON

I'm thinking about the dead girl, the one my son had known not because she was a friend—the dead girl had very few friends as it turns out, a fact that might very well have been a contributing factor to her death—but because she had attended his middle school. I've been thinking of her off and on for the last hour, and now, nearing the end of a twenty-mile bike ride, I'm remembering how, the day before, the people of my town had known the girl was missing, and that while life is rarely kind to children who have disappeared, many of us were still holding out hope that she might be found. And she was. Only she wasn't alive. Which meant that this girl, the one who, for days, had been known to us as The Missing Girl or That Girl Who'd Gone Missing, had become, in an instant, That Girl Who Was Killed or The Girl Whose Throat Had Been Slit and Whose Body Had Been Left On The Side Of The Road. However named or referenced, she was, at the very least, a human being—a pudgy redhead with a slight underbite and, if her Facebook account can be trusted to accurately represent her wardrobe, an affinity for camouflage hoodies; a girl whose time on earth ended after a brief thirteen years. The police had gathered information that led them to believe that two first-year engineering students, both of whom were enrolled at the university for which our town is known, had met at a local fast food restaurant to plan the murder, which they then executed. A year before, a news station had chosen one of these students—the same young man who would befriend the thirteen-year-old girl on a sketchy social media app that helped him trick the girl into believing that he was her boyfriend, and as such could be trusted to love and care for her—as "Athlete of the Week," and in an interview with the station the would-be killer had discussed his accomplishments as a star of track and field. During the segment, the young man, who had set a number of state records, said that he believed he could do anything he set his mind to. It was that particular phrase—*anything he set his mind to*—that I've since been unable to forget, and it's one I now replay in my head as I zip though puddles, dodging melted slush, wondering if, in the days following last week's blizzard, the dead girl had made a snowman, or if she'd sledded, or if she'd licked the ice crystals from her gloves, or if she'd pulled out her cell phone in order to prove to another person her age that she did indeed have an eighteen-year-old boyfriend, and that she planned to someday run away with him and start a family of her own. I wonder now if anyone had believed her, or if, when she'd shown them the boy's wholesome-looking face, they'd rolled their eyes and thought *here we go again with the obviously made-up shit this obnoxious girl so relentlessly peddles.* I wonder what those people think now. I think about yesterday, the worst and last day of the girl's life, which, as it happened, had been a very good day for me. I had spent the morning packing boxes for my family's subsequent move across town, to a smaller but more solidly built and more expensive home, one that had been recently and completely remodeled, and whose features include granite countertops, wood floors, a brick patio, a fenced-in backyard, and an outdoor fireplace. And as I was packing and envisioning what it would be like to live in a house where you could stand near a window in

winter and not feel the cold seeping through the poorly in-
sulated fenestration, my wife appeared at my office door
and wanted to know if, since our son was walking the dog,
I wanted to go upstairs with her. I said something like, "But
he won't be gone that long" and she said, "Well, we don't
need that much time," and because my wife is almost always right, and because it had been a while since we'd gone
upstairs together, I followed her. Afterwards, I said, "That
was a good idea" and she said, "It was, wasn't it," and then,
in the throes of afterglow, my body pulsed with gratitude.
That evening, I prepared dinner—meatballs, tomatoes, and
garlic over polenta, garnished with roasted broccolini—using a recipe and ingredients that had been shipped to us via
the United Parcel Service, and it was very good. Our son
went to sleep early because he was tired from having played
three games of indoor soccer and soon after he went to bed
my wife texted me from upstairs in our home to say she too
was turning in. I didn't remind myself about the missing
girl, didn't think that I should appreciate every last moment
with those I loved, didn't go upstairs to say goodnight to
either my wife or son face to face or to hug and kiss them
as I usually do, mostly because I was downstairs in our guest
bedroom gripping a controller, directing my avatar—a
biracial young woman in tiger-striped pants and a black
hoodie, whose face I'd paid a virtual stylist 500 virtual dollars to paint a tropical pink stripe across, for no other reason than I thought it might seem startling when I joined
other players online during heists—across town in a stolen
vehicle, to shoot at gang members who were cursing at me
in Spanish. If I died, as I sometimes did, I always came
back to life, to lay waste to thugs and afterwards retrieve
piles of cash that flew from their bodies and pulsed radio-
actively on the concrete, as did packets of drugs, which I

then delivered to an African-American man named Gerald, a tubby, bearded guy who wore a necklace over his T-shirt and who lived in an apartment complex in a part of town where, if you randomly fired your weapon, the surrounding neighbors would pull out their guns and unleash a barrage of bullets in your direction. Gerald took the package and said, "Don't you tell nobody about me now, you hear?"— which is what he always said, even though I never had told anyone, ever, and then MISSION PASSED appeared on the screen, and I watched the dollar amount—mine—rapidly rise. Finally, I texted my wife "ok" and then "night night" and she texted back "nighter," which is short for "nighter nighter chicken fighter," which is a phrase she or my son made up, and which they think is funny to say, and so I kept on playing my game until the hour grew late enough for me to worry about the total amount of sleep I'd likely be getting, after which I crept through the darkness to bed, where I slept until morning. Upon waking, I turned on my phone and discovered that the missing girl was now dead. And once I had finished reading about her suspected killers, and how they made several trips to a local Walmart, to purchase a shovel and cleaning products, I went into the next room, to check on my own child, who, I realized, had been unconscious for twelve hours. I had no reason to believe he would die peacefully in his sleep at age thirteen, but even so, the sight of his breast rising and falling was a relief, and the first thing I said once he woke was, "Do you know that girl who went missing?" and he said, "Yeah," and I said, "They found her," and he said, "They did?" and I said, "Yes. She's dead. Somebody slit her throat and dumped her body on the side of the road," and my son said, "That's awful." And I said nothing, because I wanted the information to sink in, wanted to provide my son with the opportunity to acknowledge that the world in which he lives is a home where terrible things happen that we cannot comprehend. It is this same incomprehensibility—the unfair and ghastly throat-slitting of a young girl—that I'm thinking of now as I pedal my bike. Rain is misting my face and slowly melting mounds of snow, which is seeping into the ground, creating muck and dirt, and shiny areas on the road that I worry will cause my wheels to slide out from under me, and I am cold and tired and splattered with grime after riding over miles and miles of countryside. I wonder why the missing girl had to die and how were her parents preventing themselves from storming the jail to inflict their own brand of renegade vengeance and what drives a person to kill, to methodically and with such care and patience plan the demise of a fellow human being, in this case to select one of our community's most vulnerable children and to create with the aid of modern technology a scenario in which this child would willingly barricade her door with a dresser and climb out her bedroom window and into the arms of a person who, unbeknownst to her, planned to slice open her body and let her life drain out. And it's here—in the middle of my predictably feeble quest for answers, for figuring out the why and how the girl had to die—that a heron appears, out of nowhere: a sudden cipher overhead. I recognize the familiar angular wings, the S of its neck, the vaguely pterodactyl-like form. It's beautiful to watch—the graceful flight of an ungainly bird—and for a moment I imagine what it must be like above the world, knifing through air, gliding forward without kindness or empathy. But then the bird disappears behind a stand of trees, and I am back in my own earthbound body, pedaling furiously this last too long stretch of road to get home.

# THE NEW YOU

Stops avoiding reflection in mirror. Stares self down. Busts out scale. Completes fifty push-ups. Pledges to repeat this act every morning and evening, then—with the kind of physical determination often associated with less-complacent generations—does. Shaves regularly. Keeps nose clean. Stays, for most part, out of sun. Admits wrongs. Articulates ideas in humorous and self-deprecating manner. Flosses. Scrubs tub-grunge on weekly basis, using expensive but environmentally friendly product. Changes light bulbs to the spiraling, long-lasting, energy-efficient kind. Deleafs gutters. Calls guy about yard, makes grass once again green. Removes shoes before entering house, even when retrieving, at last minute, wallet and/or keys. Knows exact location of wallet and/or keys at all times, forevermore. Per spouse's request, rinses dishes before placing them in dishwasher, despite the fact that this seems ultimately like dishwasher's job. Closes cupboards. Calls mother frequently, for no other reason than mother enjoys hearing son's voice. Remembers, before retiring each and every night, to lock all entrances to house. Leaps up, when strange sound wakes spouse in middle of night and—instead of rolling over and saying, "It's probably nothing"—carries Louisville Slugger on tour of every room. Takes preventative measures to ensure body does not become (as illustrated by certain television commercials) a house infested by anthropomorphic, monster-faced germs wearing fedoras and carrying briefcases. Purchases craft beer when hosting neighborhood poker games, eats less Frito Lay French Onion Dip and fewer Sea Salt Chips than any other player, plays conservatively, never loses everything. In general, loses less. Figures out where socks went and keeps them from going there again. Learns to change oil in car. Changes oil in car. Successfully identifies all plant life in neighborhood. Builds successful fruit fly trap. Refines beat-boxing routine. Practices and finally masters Michael Jackson dance sequence from famous live "Billie Jean" TV performance. Uses a Kleenex, for the love of Pete. Plays soccer with son and—for once—refuses to use body to overpower boy, thus ensuring game does not end—as it has, historically—in tears. Discontinues cable. Calls guy about rotten siding. Calls chimney sweep. Calls termite guy. Calls tree guys to prune limbs, thus insuring health of trees and lawn. Patronizes local farmer's market. Ceases to be territorial when preparing food. Changes diet from mostly cheese-egg-bread-sugar-and-meat-based to heart-healthy Mediterranean. Seduces spouse, not with chocolate or roses or poses thought to be hilariously sexy but by being generally helpful and pleasant, returning things to proper places, cleaning house from top to bottom, avoiding garlic, and in general separating order from chaos. Goes paperless. Successfully avoids reading any and all user comments on any and all websites. Refuses to mock adherents of now-abandoned and largely misunderstood denomination to which nearly every other family member belongs. Stops googling sermons of uncle, who happens to be the president of said denomination, and thus stops shaking head and rolling eyes at message that seems more and more to be like a professionally crafted sales pitch for World's Most Reasonable Cult. Gratefully embraces memories of former worldview wherein planet presided over by giant human-shaped God, to whom no request was ever too small, and who mandated that humans refrain from work and secular activities on seventh day of week. Successfully integrates all knowledge—of science, history, religion, language, music, and culture—into unified, evolving, many-splendored theory of reality. Practices meditation. Travels—thanks to instructions via book on shamanism and mp3 of Native American drumming—from ordinary to non-ordinary reality, finds spirit animal, then regularly and without irony consults it on personal matters. Keeps beliefs to self. Refuses to proselytize or judge. Performs herbal cleanse. Charts progress. Says, "Just water, thanks" while staring at photo of jumbo margarita. Chooses salad instead of fries, kale chips instead of potato. Collects all coins in house, drives them to grocery store, pays a machine to count them, trades them in for paper, donates bills to homeless guy with cardboard sign on side of road. Plants garden, reaps bountiful harvest. Figures out kid's math homework, how to add or subtract or multiply or divide in a non-regular way, so kid can learn and appreciate version of math that was devised for children who possess learning styles that may or may not describe his own. Practices—and masters—that one Bach piece in "I Used to Know How to Play Piano" book. Stops using plastic bags, except for biodegradable ones provided for pet excrement by plastic green stands along neighborhood trail system. Walks dog for full hour every day (regardless of blistering heat or blizzardlike conditions) while listening to lectures from that Great Courses place that advertises in *Harper's Magazine*. Actually reads *Harper's Magazine* but also, for sake of balance, *National Review*. Learns basics of Arabic, Spanish, and Mandarin. Purchases life insurance. Contributes to kid's college fund. Meets with rep at bank to start mutual fund. Trades stocks with confidence. Calls Volvo dealership and receives radio code (now required for radio to work, after battery died) so as to listen not to the prognostication of arrogant douchebags concerning professional athletes who just wanna give all the glory to Jesus but to "Morning Classics." Successfully convinces spouse to deactivate landline. Adds date of Hazardous Household to iPhone calendar, sets alert, finally gets detergent bottles sloshing with old gas out of garage. Takes weekly 24-hour break from all electronics. Spends regular time in woods, notes that—despite headlines about students shooting teachers or stolen passwords or drug snorting celebs or World's Most Corrupt Nation—flora and fauna remain, as ever, themselves: silent, delicate, lovely, and inscrutable. Switches from coffee to tea, sugar to honey. Says prayer for collapsing bee colonies. Purchases road bike and bib and pair of Shimano shoes that lock into pedals. Overcomes self-consciousness inspired by getup, rides bike twenty miles a day, sheds fifteen pounds. Survives accident, signs new lease on life. Makes list of unread works of classical literature, reads one per week for rest of life. Studies and finally "gets" physics. Memorizes constellations. Signs up for self-defense course. Deactivates Facebook account, uses spouse's to troll, but only on Saturday mornings. Purchases new underwear. Chooses new ring tone—one that doesn't reveal some essential and regrettable quality about personal preferences. Lounges, without guilt or shame, in blanket with sleeves. Grows old in golden light falling upon western mountains. Paddles canoe. Casts lines. Takes bath in claw foot tub in middle of forest. Places finger on the pulse. Keeps it there. Whispers the numbers. Counts.

# LIFTOFF

I was afraid of liftoff. Afraid what the sudden shift in altitude might do to my ears, which had been clogged for weeks—since Thanksgiving, actually—with fluid, a condition that had greatly impaired my hearing and caused me, in certain claustrophobic moments, to feel as though I was on the verge of a panic attack. I'd been to an ear, nose, and throat guy the day before, a young doctor who, after I removed my hoodie so the nurse could take my blood pressure, had eyeballed my natty T-shirt—the one emblazoned with the letters "USA" and the iconic Olympic rings—and asked me if I was a competitor, though he likely knew the answer to that question. The doctor then pointed to a map on the wall of the human inner ear and informed me that what most people thought of the ear—the visible fleshy part—was really simply an amplifier and that the process of translating sound took place inside, where a complicated group of twisty shapes collaborated to send sounds to the brain. He then prescribed a hearing test—it would be, he assured me, an X-ray for my ears—and so I exited the examination room and sat down in a waiting area alongside a very old man who had a scar running down the side of his head. Eventually, I was summoned to a soundproof booth, where a woman—one whose tan, wrinkled face made me think she must have lived a life in which the smoking of cigarettes acted as a frequent punctuation in her daily routine—provided me with a pair of headphones and a handheld mechanism whose trigger I was instructed to press every time I heard a beep. I heard beeps but they quickly grew faint, sometimes so much so that I worried I might be imagining them, and thereby contribute to an inaccurate reading. The doctor's "X-ray" metaphor seemed to me something of a stretch, especially if we were relying as much as I assumed we were on human interpretation. The smoker lady then asked me to repeat a string of words she pronounced, like "birthday" and "baseball" and "sidewalk" and "downtown," and some other words I couldn't hear because each time her voice receded a little further into oblivion. Once we had finished, the doctor read the test, and explained that I did indeed have some partial hearing loss, and though this would likely be restored, and I could expect the problem to resolve itself in ninety days or less, he could cut an incision in each eardrum and then drain out the fluid, a relatively painless procedure that would hopefully ensure that I could avoid what might otherwise be, thanks to the increased air pressure inside the cabin of an airplane, an exquisite kind of agony. I didn't like the idea of a knife entering my ear canal and cutting something open in there, but I also didn't like the idea of a sustained and exquisite agony, so I agreed to the procedure. I sat in a chair that reminded me of a dentist's and almost made a comment about my father being a dentist but didn't want to postpone the inevitable. When it was over—after the doctor had made his incisions, each of which represented two scorching dots of pain deep inside my head, and after he had drained out the fluid—I nearly cried because nothing seemed to have changed, my ears still felt full, and I could still hear my voice in my head when I spoke. The doctor said, "Huh," and "Well, I don't know what to tell you." And then in the car, I did cry, a little, and I felt

stupid and weak and childish, but I couldn't help imagining what it would be like if this clogged ear situation
represented the tip of the iceberg in terms of my suffering,
if this condition wasn't temporary but was instead the beginning of a slow decline in terms of my hearing, that
maybe I'd be a forty-three-year-old with a giant hearing
aid, at least until the sense disappeared completely, and
then I'd have to learn sign language, probably lose my job
because I needed my ears, relied on them while teaching
almost every minute of class, though maybe I could claim
disability and because of some kind of diversity initiative
I couldn't be fired but instead would be included in a tally
of the ways my university was inclusive, a notch on the
belt of their own contributions to diversity and inclusion.
I was thinking about all of this as I sat on the plane, which,
as usual, was small and the seating cramped and had been
sitting for what seemed to be far too long upon the tar-
mac. Our flight attendant was a tall black woman with
square glasses and as we prepared for liftoff she buckled
herself in a seat facing the cabin. It struck me that she resembled a grownup version of the avatar I created for *Grand
Theft Auto*, an orange-haired, sunglasses-wearing, Mo-
hawked woman who wore a hoodie and tiger-striped leg-
gings. I don't know why I created her except maybe in my
mind I thought this fucked-up universe I was about to
enter needed a hero that didn't look like me, so I created
her and named her Metatron, after the angel who led the
Israelites out of Egypt, though that moniker got lost when
I transferred her character from Xbox to PlayStation, and
somehow ended up with my Rockstar email address, which
is a combination of my and my son's initials. Unfortu-
nately, the fact that our stewardess looked like a badass
offered little comfort to me, as I had the whole ears and

exquisite pain thing to contend with. I put my phone on airplane mode, and tried to distract myself, tried to envision New York City, which was my destination, but instead I found myself thinking of the President-Elect and his cabinet, a veritable rogue's gallery of the rich and powerful, and how the President-Elect was like Satan summoning the beasts of Revelation, except instead of seven-headed leopards and bears with horns we got old white men who were being primed to lead agencies whose very existence they opposed. Perhaps because I had a general a sense of impending doom, I remembered the morning of September 11th, 2001, which, I suppose you could say that I remember as clearly as if it were yesterday, and in some respects, more clearly than yesterday. On that morning, I was sitting in the living room of the duplex where I lived in Lafayette, Indiana, at a cheap Walmart desk, laptop open, working on a story that took the form of a will and testament. The phone rang, and moments later my wife, who had just gotten out of the shower, entered the room to tell me that her sister, who lived in Savannah, Georgia, had called to say that terrorists had hijacked airplanes and crashed them into the World Trade Center. My first thought was: *no way*. My wife assured me it was true, and that her sister had seen the replay of the event on TV. We didn't have a television in the house— my wife was a PhD candidate in Purdue University, where I worked as a teacher of first-year writing, and our combined annual gross income was less than thirty grand, and cable seemed like a luxury we couldn't afford—so I ended up driving a few blocks away, to our friend Arron and Cathy's place, a house that smelled to me like somebody's grandparents', perhaps because everything Arron and Cathy owned—couches and lamps and bookshelves stuffed with old hardbacks—were at least fifty years old. There, in a room filled with the things of the past, I watched a transmission that seemed to be arriving from an alternate future reality: the unfathomable collapse of skyscrapers, a cascade of rubble that churned a doomsday cloud into the sky. Later that day, I sat in the tiny green yard outside our tiny white house. It was, as it had been in Manhattan, a beautiful day, the cloudless sky a deep blue. I didn't know what to think. I assumed life would never be the same. Everything I had done, or would do, or could think of to do, seemed embarrassingly trivial. What was the point of writing stories, or teaching students how to consider audience, purpose, and rhetorical situation when writing essays? We lived in a world where desperate maniacs had come out of nowhere and used our own technology to slay thousands of people? What would happen next? How were any of us supposed to live? It may sound melodramatic to say, but I had experienced a similar feeling on the morning of November 9, 2016, when I turned on my phone and saw the name of our new President-Elect. Our nation, which had the chance to elect its first female president, had chosen a bully, a sexual predator, a failed businessman. I know that there are people who say that Obama didn't fulfill his promise as a progressive liberal, that he didn't dissolve Guantanamo, that he okayed drone strikes that ended up killing civilians. But I liked him. I liked having him as president. I liked knowing that he and Michelle invited intellectuals to private dinners, or that he'd befriended Marilynne Robinson, with whom he published a conversation about literature and books and citizenship in *The New York Review of Books*. I liked that he had a sense of humor, that he could roast somebody and that he could himself take a good ribbing, that he was capable of self-deprecation. I'm not stupid. I know his success is due in part to his charisma and charm, and that those things aren't worth nearly as much as courage and honor, but you could count on him to respond to tragic events—Sandy Hook, the shooting of Trayvon Martin, the riots in Ferguson—with a calm and nuanced resolve. I didn't care if in secret he had gone mad with power—though honestly I find that very difficult to imagine, in part because he stood up for things that I cared about, and championed programs and initiatives that would help those who were less fortunate, or who lived at the fringes of our society, or were shunned and denied rights by self-righteous fundamentalists. So waking up knowing that we had replaced one of our most literary presidents with one of our most illiterate was, to say the very least, disorienting. The sense I had of the country I lived in had dissolved. I didn't know, for instance, what to tell my students, many of whom, I knew, could not abide the idea of a President-Elect who had once bragged about grabbing women by their genitals. So I didn't tell them anything. In my Contemporary Fiction class, we'd spent the previous two months talking about received narratives—the stories we've been told by others about what it means to be alive—and we'd been reading stories and books by writers who were willing to turn our expectations about what it meant to tell a story on its head. Watching them engage with these texts, watching them struggle to understand why an author would end a story without resolving—at least to their satisfaction—the book's main question, or why an author would forgo sensory description and figurative language in favor of speaking simply and directly to a reader, was not unlike watching the androids on HBO's *Westworld* awake to the narratives that they'd been programmed to think of as real. The day after the election, I told the class that we weren't going to talk about the novel we'd been studying—the one written by an Asian guy from Brooklyn who'd been celebrated in so-called alt-lit circles, and which detailed a relationship between a twenty-two-year-old writer and the sixteen-year-old girl he was dating, and included transcripts of their online chats, during which they talked about shoplifting, suicide, eating vegan foods, and whether a colony of ants could defeat Bruce Lee—we were going to write about what had happened over the last twenty-four hours; though most students wrote what they had to say within thirty minutes and left, one young woman wrote for the entire class period, and then thanked me afterwards, which, I'll admit, struck me as strange, since she could've written at any time, didn't have to be in a classroom to write, although perhaps she was simply relieved that someone in charge—someone she had to answer to, more or less—had taken the time to recognize that maybe she *needed* to write, and carving out that space where she could unleash her anger and sadness, handing in a stack of pages that were ribbed where the pressure of her pen had created furious little furrows, was essential to being able to move forward, because what else was there to do? I thought of my students as the plane's wheels started to roll again, and because I myself didn't know what else to do, I took out a notebook of my own, and as I felt the little surge that accompanies leaving the ground, I began, with no small amount of trepidation, to write.

## Acknowledgments

The author is grateful to the following magazines where many of these subsequently appeared:

*Autre*: "Fat Kid";
*Booth*: "Blood Soup";
*Boulevard*: "Cult Hymn";
*The Brooklyn Rail*: "Status Update," "Hatchling," "Last Blood," "Robocall," "Can't Feel My Face," "33rd Balloon," "Fool's Gold," "Top Secret," "Holy Hours," and "Bring Me the Head of Geraldo Rivera";
*The Collagist*: "Sinkhole";
*Copper Nickel*: "Heron";
*The Fanzine*: "Brain Bank";
*Flyway*: "Land of Enchantment," "Tiger Moth," and "Inferno";
*Hot Metal Bridge*: "Well of Souls" and "Signs of the Times";
*Juked*: "Precious Metals," "Permanent Exhibit," and "Treasure Box";
*LitMag*: "We All Go into the Dark";
*New Orleans Review*: "Black Magic" and "Trick-or-Treat";
*Okey-Panky*: "Night Thoughts";
*The Scofield*: "Hands Up," "Observatorium," "Stormbox," "Game Day," and "Eye of the Storm";
*Sonora Review*: "The New You";
*Washington Square*: "Source Material";
*Willow Springs*: "Gong Bang Cleanse."

## About the Author

Matthew Vollmer is the author of two collections of short fiction—*Gateway to Paradise* (Persea, 2015) and *Future Missionaries of America* (MacAdam/Cage, 2009; Salt Publishing, 2010)—as well as a collection of essays, each written in the form of an epitaph—*inscriptions for headstones* (Outpost19, 2012). His work has appeared widely, in such places as *Paris Review, Glimmer Train, Tin House, Ploughshares, StoryQuarterly, Virginia Quarterly Review, Epoch, Ecotone, New England Review, DIAGRAM, Colorado Review, Hayden's Ferry Review, The Normal School, Willow Springs, The Antioch Review, Gulf Coast, The Collagist, Carolina Quarterly, Oxford American, The Sun, Best American Essays*, and *The Pushcart Prize Anthology*. With David Shields, he co-edited *FAKES: An Anthology of Pseudo-Interviews, Faux-Lectures, Quasi-Letters, "Found" Texts, and Other Fraudulent Artifacts* (W. W. Norton, 2012). He also served as editor for *The Book of Uncommon Prayer* (Outpost19, 2015), an anthology of everyday invocations featuring the work of over sixty writers. He teaches at Virginia Tech and lives in Blacksburg, Virginia, with his wife, son, cat, and dog.

# BOA Editions, Ltd. American Reader Series

No. 1    *Christmas at the Four Corners of the Earth*
Prose by Blaise Cendrars
Translated by Bertrand Mathieu

No. 2    *Pig Notes & Dumb Music: Prose on Poetry*
By William Heyen

No. 3    *After-Images: Autobiographical Sketches*
By W. D. Snodgrass

No. 4    *Walking Light: Memoirs and Essays on Poetry*
By Stephen Dunn

No. 5    *To Sound Like Yourself: Essays on Poetry*
By W. D. Snodgrass

No. 6    *You Alone Are Real to Me: Remembering Rainer Maria Rilke*
By Lou Andreas-Salomé

No. 7    *Breaking the Alabaster Jar: Conversations with Li-Young Lee*
Edited by Earl G. Ingersoll

No. 8    *I Carry A Hammer In My Pocket For Occasions Such As These*
By Anthony Tognazzini

No. 9    *Unlucky Lucky Days*
By Daniel Grandbois

No. 10    *Glass Grapes and Other Stories*
By Martha Ronk

No. 11    *Meat Eaters & Plant Eaters*
By Jessica Treat

No. 12    *On the Winding Stair*
By Joanna Howard

No. 13    *Cradle Book*
By Craig Morgan Teicher

No. 14    *In the Time of the Girls*
By Anne Germanacos

No. 15    *This New and Poisonous Air*
By Adam McOmber

No. 16 *To Assume a Pleasing Shape*
By Joseph Salvatore

No. 17 *The Innocent Party*
By Aimee Parkison

No. 18 *Passwords Primeval: 20 American Poets in Their Own Words*
Interviews by Tony Leuzzi

No. 19 *The Era of Not Quite*
By Douglas Watson

No. 20 *The Winged Seed: A Remembrance*
By Li-Young Lee

No. 21 *Jewelry Box: A Collection of Histories*
By Aurelie Sheehan

No. 22 *The Tao of Humiliation*
By Lee Upton

No. 23 *Bridge*
By Robert Thomas

No. 24 *Reptile House*
By Robin McLean

No. 25 *The Education of a Poker Player*
James McManus

No. 26 *Remarkable*
By Dinah Cox

No. 27 *Gravity Changes*
By Zach Powers

No. 28 *My House Gathers Desires*
By Adam McOmber

No. 29 *An Orchard in the Street*
By Reginald Gibbons

No. 30 *The Science of Lost Futures*
By Ryan Habermeyer

No. 31 *Permanent Exhibit*
By Matthew Vollmer

# Colophon

BOA Editions, Ltd., a not-for-profit publisher of poetry and other literary works, fosters readership and appreciation of contemporary literature. By identifying, cultivating, and publishing both new and established poets and selecting authors of unique literary talent, BOA brings high-quality literature to the public. Support for this effort comes from the sale of its publications, grant funding, and private donations.

•

*The publication of this book is made possible, in part, by the special support of the following individuals:*

Anonymous
Angela Bonazinga & Catherine Lewis
Chris & DeAnna Cebula
Gwen & Gary Conners
Marjorie F. Grinols
Gouvernet Arts Fund
Art & Pam Hatton
Sandi Henschel
Jack & Gail Langerak
Joe McElveney
Dan Meyers, *in honor of J. Shepard Skiff*
Boo Poulin
Deborah Ronnen & Sherman Levey
Steven O. Russell & Phyllis Rifkin-Russell
Sue S. Stewart, *in memory of Stephen L. Raymond*
Allan & Melanie Ulrich
William Waddell & Linda Rubel,
*in honor of Simah, Ethan, and Jeehye*